Achieving Prosperity Through Diversity

How to Embrace, Support, and Lead a Diverse Cultural Workforce

Gobinder Gill

Achieving Prosperity Through Diversity:
How to Embrace, Support, and Lead a Diverse Cultural Workforce

ISBN 10: 1-933817-60-7
ISBN 13: 978-1-933817-60-6

Published by: Expert Author Publishing
http://expertauthorpublishing.com

Canadian Address:
501- 1155 The High Street,
Coquitlam, BC, Canada
V3B.7W4
Phone: (604) 941-3041
Fax: (604) 944-7993

US Address:
1300 Boblett Street
Unit A-218
Blaine, WA 98230
Phone: (866) 492-6623
Fax: (250) 493-6603

Table of Contents

Dedication

To my late mother, Rachpal Kaur, even at an early age in my dreams, I knew you were near and could hear your laughter. Also for my late grandmother, Sham Kaur, who taught me the value of forgiveness. In addition, for my fourth-grade teacher, Brian Waplington, whose deep caring always gave me hope and desire to succeed in life.

Foreword

I believe North America's rapidly changing workforce is seeking answers to new economic questions.

At this point in time, businesses are at the crossroads of a new economic phenomenon: new professional immigrants will be the driving workforce in the modern Western business world. It is certain that this new and ambitious trend will need answers from individuals with similar experiences.

My past twenty-five years of extensive experiences in the mainstream and ethnic media (radio, television, film, and print) have taught me that it is important to be receptive to this new, tremendous business opportunity.

Successful businesses need to be aware of this exciting and challenging period in the modern workforce. If the businesses are not open-minded in their new strategies and new emerging market, they will miss the golden opportunity of the twenty-first century.

Inside the pages of this book, you will learn how to recruit, train, and retain a diverse workforce in the modern workplace.

It's my greatest passion to help other businesses thrive and achieve diversity; to emphasize the necessity for being proactive when approaching our global marketplace; and to help everyone embrace, think about, feel, and believe in a diverse workplace.

Sincerely,
Gobinder Gill
info@gobindergill.com
www.gobindergill.com

Introduction

"Diversity isn't something you ought to have. It's something you need to have."

-When Generations Collide

Today there is very little argument against diversity being an essential component for any company to remain successful in the ever-changing global business market.

Practically every business requires new techniques to take full advantage of the opportunities discussed in this book, whether operating domestically or worldwide.

When it comes to any business decisions or strategies, diversity is one of the main elements that must to be kept at the forefront.

At the end of the day, a corporation's diversity policy affects its revenue.

The main question any company nccds to ask itself is, "How is diversity, or the lack thereof, affecting our productivity and profits?"

For many people, diversity is something that's taken for granted. Take a look wherever you are—the sidewalks, stores, and neighborhoods are filled with people from all cultural backgrounds and racial diversities.

But is it the same in the workplace?

Before you answer, there are some ideas to consider. In many companies, diversity is nothing more than window dressing. Companies might have a few minorities or some written diversity policy, yet perhaps they're not fully embracing diversity and all of the benefits a diverse workforce provides.

<u>The goal of this book isn't to point fingers.</u>

Rather, the goal is to help companies, hiring managers, business owners, board members, and leaders to realize the positive impact a diverse workforce offers. The goal is to offer tangible steps and strategies to embrace that diverse workforce.

The topic of diversity can be a heavy-handed and intense conversation.

That is not our objective here.

The power of this book lies in a focus on the positive steps everyone can take to optimize the benefits of diversity.

The first aspect is to realize that diversity in workplaces and neighborhoods is standard. It is here to stay and prosper.

This is a great thing!

Right now diversity provides a powerful opportunity to initiate imaginative changes to any company's bottom line.

Exploring the Myriad Opportunities Diversity Offers

- The labor workforce demographics are shifting quickly. As the world changes and grows, the workplace must too. It ought to reflect the world culturally, economically, and socially. When a workforce is out of sync with the world around it, progress and innovation are stunted.
- The converse is also true. When the demographics reflect the outside world and increasing globalization, business owners and managers are better in tune with trends and are thus ready to adapt, innovate, and prosper.
- When we talk about diversity, it's not just cultural diversity we're referring to. Take a look at the workforce fifty years ago and you'll see that it was fairly homogenous. You had a primarily white, male workforce.
- Today, people of all ages, religions, ethnic backgrounds, races, sexual orientation, disabilities, skills, and levels of education work together to bring about a dynamic workforce. This

creates a fertile breeding ground for thoughts, ideas, opinions, and even systems of belief to improve and grow a business.

- While we're all different, when you only have one perspective, growth and innovation move at a much slower pace and adapting to our rapidly changing world sometimes just doesn't happen.
- Anticipations of consumers and workers have changed. They have also changed as to where most of us are employed. This continues to shift along with who supplies the service, what the service is, and how the service is provided. A diverse workforce allows you to stay in tune with changes and adapt quickly. It gives you a competitive edge.

> "The survival of the fittest is the ageless law of nature, but the fittest are rarely the strong. The fittest are those endowed with the qualifications for adaptation, the ability to accept the inevitable and conform to the unavoidable, to harmonize with existing or changing conditions."

- Technology has likewise changed today's workplace. Some organizations, however, are not taking advantage of the amazing benefits technology offers a growing enterprise. They might be managing to make payroll and holding onto their current clientele, but they are not growing.

  Why do they resist change? Is it fear, ignorance, or a lack of time and leadership? Whatever it is, however, it is detrimental to the health of the organization, and severely hinders its growth. On the other hand, those who embrace technology and keep up with the changing times will thrive. It is the same for companies who embrace diversity.
- Suppliers are diverse, and in order to work together optimally, companies need internal representation, understanding, and support.
- Business is becoming ever more global, and the world is indeed

a diverse place. Think about the marketplace as it is today. One small business owner can do business with people all around the globe—from Canada to Egypt, from Australia to India. It pays to have a staff equipped and trained to communicate effectively with all walks of life.

Powerful and competitive companies know:

That broadening your horizons is essential. Cultural diversity must be looked upon as an opportunity. A diverse staff knows what kind of merchandise is required in places that you may never go to. Are you aware as to what sells in certain parts of India, Turkey, and China? If not, a diverse team of employees probably will.

That diversity is about more than embracing it internally with policies and procedures. Customers are diverse, and in order to understand and meet their needs, we need inside representation, acknowledgment, and support.

That diversity is about more than positive action. It's about understanding prejudice (our own and others); it's about discussion, education, compassion, and a genuine effort to change corporate missions, visions, and strategies.

Embracing Diversity is Not as Easy as it Sounds

Workplace diversity refers to embracing, supporting, and, in fact, seeking the variety of differences between people in an organization.

That sounds simple, but diversity encompasses race, gender, ethnic group, age, personality, cognitive style, tenure, organizational function, education, background, and more.

Diversity takes into account not just how individuals perceive others but how they view themselves. Those perceptions affect their communications and relations with others. For many employees to function effectively, human resource professionals, managers, and business leaders need to communicate effectively on issues involving flexibility, and change.

> **As the world shrinks and globalization prevails, diversity will increase significantly in the coming years.**

Successful companies are aware of the need for immediate action and are ready and willing to allocate resources for managing diversity in the workplace right now.

Are you?

This book is devoted to not only helping you build and maintain a diverse workforce, but also to helping you recognize and take advantage of this amazing opportunity. Before we jump into the first chapter, let's explore the simple benefits and challenges to employing a diverse workforce.

When We Embrace Diversity as a Fundamental Mission, the Benefits are Astounding

You will:

- Attract, recruit, and retain individuals from a wide "talent" background.
- Minimize the costs of labor turnover, productivity, and absenteeism.
- Gain better staff flexibility and responsiveness.
- Increase staff commitment and self-confidence.
- Enhance creativity and innovation.

- Improve understanding of how to operate effectively in different cultures and markets.
- Improve understanding of the needs of current customers.
- Improve company knowledge about the needs of new clients.
- Expand new products, services, and marketing policies.
- Improve your reputation and image inside your community.

The rewards truly are astonishing and profitable!

Making Workplace Diversity a Priority

Your success and ability to compete in an increasingly global market depend on your ability to embrace diversity and realize its benefits.

However, companies can't simply snap their fingers and say they're diverse. Diversity happens through a comprehensive and systematic shift. It begins with the very top-level managers and employees and trickles down to include each and every employee. It's about changing policies and procedures to support diversity, it's about education, and it's about assessment and evaluation.

We're each independently responsible for making a larger change. It begins by assessing and discussing our own personal beliefs, biases, and stereotypes. It begins with honesty. And it ends with prosperity and a global and diverse workforce, which supports innovation, recognition, and growth.

An organization that embraces diversity at its core receives:

- An ability to adapt quickly to changes in the marketplace.
- An ability to offer products and services to a broader clientele.
- An ability to tap into creativity and innovation.
- An ability to execute and respond quickly and appropriately to challenges.

It's Not All Smiles and Hand Clapping

There are many challenges to diversity in the workplace.

Think about how difficult it is to speak to someone in a calm and rational manner when you believe they've just disrespected you and your culture. Heated exchanges can and do happen.

There are many barriers to overcome, including:

- Communication barriers.
- Perception barriers.
- Stereotypes and biases.
- Resistance to change.

The goal of this book is to help companies overcome these challenges! Throughout this book, we'll take a look at:

- Defining diversity – looking beyond race.
- Developing positive and proactive diversity strategies.
- Bias-free staffing.
- Effective leadership.
- Retaining a multicultural workforce.
- Avoiding and understanding stereotypes.
- What an ideal workforce might look like.

This book is for you if:

- You're an executive responsible for maintaining your company's competitive advantage.
- You're a manager who wants more cohesive working groups.
- You're a human resources professional who wants to improve ethnic representation in your company.

- You're a salesperson who is interested in tapping into new global markets.
- You're an employee or manager who wants to enhance your workplace environment and overall company satisfaction.
- You're a person who is looking for a job and faces discrimination, bias, and stereotyping.

This book also offers tips for new immigrants who are trying to break into the workforce in the Western world. And finally, we discuss some multicultural etiquettes and offer tips for Westerners working abroad.

This book is intended for all corporations and companies that want to succeed in the ever-changing global market of the twenty-first century.

Let's get started!

Chapter One – What Is Diversity, Really?

"[People] may be said to resemble not the bricks of which
a house is built, but the pieces of a picture puzzle, each
differing in shape, but matching the rest, and thus bringing
out the picture."

-Felix Adler

To begin to take advantage of a global and diverse workforce, it's important to first come to a mutual definition about what diversity is.

Ask 100 different people for their definition of diversity and you're liable to receive 100 different answers. Many of these answers will reflect affirmative-action policies or address specific groups of people.

This is because when people talk about diversity they often do so from their own perspective, from their own unique experiences, which are potentially biased—actually, they're almost guaranteed to be biased.

Generally, we think of diversity as being a co-existence of various ethnic backgrounds and genders.

This definition is actually quite limited.

The reality is that a co-existence of ethnic backgrounds and genders is just the beginning of what it truly means to be in a diverse workplace.

We're each more than our gender and our ethnic background.

Now ask yourself what diversity means to you. Would you consider your current workplace to be diverse?

In order for us to be on the same page, so to speak, when discussing the power of a diverse workforce, it's important to have a working definition. This will help to create a strategy for diversity and allow properly trained management, human-resources personnel, and other employees to thrive in a diverse workforce.

Additionally, it'll help you create strategies, processes, and goals to optimize your business for future growth and profits.

A Working Definition of Diversity

In the social sphere, the concept of diversity centers on acknowledging and embracing a variety of cultural differences and similarities. These include race, ethnic backgrounds, religious faith, age, gender, sexual orientation, socio-economics and physical disabilities.

In other words, diversity includes all characteristics and experiences that define each of us as individuals.

In the workplace, however, it's all too easy to give this concept short shrift. It can be inconvenient to take the time to understand each other. Employees may worry that their employers would not want exploratory cross-cultural interactions occurring on their time.

It's up to human-resource professionals, managers, and business leaders to let them know it's okay—and, in fact, to lead the way.

> **When businesses view diversity as something more than a moral imperative, when they see it as a business opportunity, then they can begin to create a powerful, and profitable, diversity strategy.**

So now that we have a working definition of diversity, let's explore some working examples of what a diverse workplace looks like.

When Does Real Diversity in the Workplace Occur?

Real diversity takes place when it starts at the top—from the Board of Directors, officers, and senior-management levels—and works itself all the way down.

This goes beyond the mere concept of setting a good example.

There are many organizations where the mid - and lower-level employees are quite diverse; however, this is only the beginning.

In order to benefit from a diverse workforce, a business must take several initiatives, including ensuring that diversity reaches all levels of the organization, from the top down.

This is imperative, as we'll discuss in subsequent chapters, because to recruit and retain the best candidates, your organization must create an atmosphere of respect and reward.

Additionally, your company's reputation affects your ability to hire well. When you embrace diversity at all levels, and you create strategies and processes to make this happen, you'll achieve a welcome reputation in your industry and community, and you'll have a highly successful and motivated workforce. And that's what it's all about.

Real diversity occurs when it is part of your overall company philosophy.

It takes more than one person or one department to embrace and create a diverse workforce. It takes an entire company.

Everyone, from the shareholders to the lowest-paid staff, must be on board and aggressively working toward this common objective.

The initial step is to modify your mission statement and company vision to incorporate your goals and philosophy. Then strategies and initiatives, including quantifiable goals and tactics to measure success, can be put into action.

Real diversity happens when it is amongst the highest-salaried staff in the corporation.

Imagine if everyone who was of one particular race and age received the highest salaries. There's no way that would go unnoticed by other employees. People are very conscious of who makes the most money, and if there's an unfair disparity in salaries, it quickly leads to disgruntled employees.

When we discuss hiring and retaining a diverse workforce in Chapter Three, we'll talk about how a positive company image is essential to getting the best employees.

One strategy, among many, to achieve a positive image is to ensure diversity at all levels and for salaries to reflect that diversity— equal pay for equal work.

Beyond maintaining a positive company image, consider the financial drain such a low and unhappy morale would cause. No one is excited to go to work; in fact, they learn to resent being there, which means they're not excited to contribute, innovate, communicate effectively, or advance the company or their career.

On the other hand, when people know they're going to be treated fairly and compensated on merit, and that everyone, regardless of their background, is accepted and appreciated, you could end up with a tremendously powerful workforce on your hands. Then you will have limitless potential as a company.

You will have a group of people who are proud of their employer, happy to go to work, engaged at work, and contributing to the bottom line.

Real diversity happens when diversity is amongst the business's general workforce.

While sameness can be comforting, it isn't stimulating. It's actually quite dull, and that homogeneousness can and will make itself shown in productivity, morale, and profits.

Additionally, while statistics may show that a company employs people from several demographics, those statistics might not show that those employees may be relegated to a specific area of the company.

This isn't the kind of diversity that will lead to long-term success and profitability.

If the majority of the mailroom, administrative staff, shipping and receiving staff, tech support, or customer support are of a particular gender, age, ethnic group, and so on, you're essentially still perpetuating stereotypes and not embracing all that diversity has to offer.

While the goal shouldn't be to meet certain numbers or percentages in each company division and job description, the goal should be to reach out to all types of people and to hire the best person for the job, regardless of the job.

We'll discuss how to create strategies that support a diverse workforce, and how to lead it, in subsequent chapters.

Real diversity happens when hiring managers recruit in ethnic publications.

It's easy to say to yourself, "Yes, we embrace all races, religions, ethnicities, sexual orientation, ages, and genders." But your actions speak louder than your words.

Do you actually take the steps necessary to create a diverse workforce? One such step is to recruit employees via ethnic publications.

Again, be wary of stereotypes here. You don't want to target specific groups of people for specific types of jobs. This limits you and your company. Instead, post the same jobs in your chosen collection of publications, which ideally would represent a diverse group of people.

Real diversity occurs when company employees have memberships in ethnic professional organizations.

One of the benefits of a diverse workforce from the top down is that you'll have people representing all walks of life. This allows for networking in a variety of communities. It also leads directly back to having your senior professionals come from diverse backgrounds.

Your brand image and networking possibilities—both of which have a direct relationship to profits—multiply exponentially when your senior employees have diverse backgrounds, interests, and networking organizations. It also makes recruiting easier because search staff can connect with ethnic cultural professional organizations and events.

Real diversity occurs when charitable contributions and volunteer initiatives embrace various ethnic organizations.

Consider for a moment if you were an employee of a company that was fairly diverse, yet the company only donated money to breast cancer charities.

If you're a woman, this might be okay with you, but if you're a man or from a demographic that doesn't really have to deal with breast cancer, then this charitable policy may leave you frowning.

However, if the company you work for does good work in other communities and donates to charities that benefit many demographics, then you're more likely to be proud to work for them.

Consider also the immense benefit not only to your community but also to your company's image if you're actively involved in a number of charities and organizations that benefit the community as a whole.

The end result is that diversity in the workforce produces profit.

When a company creates a vision to embrace diversity and implements goals, strategies to meet those goals, and a continuing process of assessment and support, amazing things can and do happen.

Business becomes more innovative and profitable. A positive company image is attained. Employees are happier and thus turnover is significantly decreased, and it becomes easier to hire the best people.

It all begins by developing a desire for diversity.

Before an entire organization can embrace the benefits of a diverse workforce and before steps can be taken to get there, it has to be initiated.

This can be achieved by one's commitment, personal examination, one's own curiosity, and wanting to truly learn about others.

It starts with learning to embrace the differences and similarities between people.

It starts with an honest dialogue.

It starts by asking yourself:

- What do you believe to be true about other types of people?
- Is it really true?
- Where did those beliefs, biases, and stereotypes come from?
- What do you know about cultures and groups already represented in your organization?
- What are your biases and stereotypes?

Honest dialogue is just the beginning.

In order to succeed and prosper in our continually changing and growing global market, it is crucial that diversity becomes the norm in the workplace in the twenty-first century.

Consider for a moment who your main customers are. Where do they come from? How many different types of languages do they speak? What is their socioeconomic status? What are their belief systems? Chances are, you're noticing something important here—you're noticing that your clientele comes from an extremely diverse group of people.

Diversity Already Exists

Take a look around you the next time you're on a city street and you'll see an amazing amalgam of people—people from every single walk of life imaginable. The possibilities of what we can accomplish when that same diversity is brought into the workforce are endless.

Before we jump into the next chapter and begin to take a look at what it takes to develop a corporate business strategy that embraces and seeks diversity, it's important to recognize that diversity is already here.

Take a look at the following statistics:

- According to a 2011 U.S. census, one in five Americans over the age of 5 speaks a language other than English at home.
- 170 different languages are spoken in New York City.
- In Australia and the U.K., demographics point to labor forces no longer being homogeneous.
- In Canada, one in four speaks a language other than English.
- Between 2001 and 2006, Canada's visible minority population increased by 27%, five times more than growth rate overall.
- 16.25% of Canada's population are visible minorities; Vancouver and Toronto have more than 40% of the population as visible minorities.
- One in five Canadians is foreign born.
- Canada's prosperity depends on an immigrant population to fill vacant positions.
- When it comes to acceptance of diversity, Canada and Australia, along with Sweden, followed in distance when compared to the U.S. and the U.K.
- Women held 49.83% of the 132 million jobs in the U.S. in June, 2009 and they're gaining the vast majority of jobs in the few sectors of the economy that are growing, according to the most recent numbers available from the Bureau of Labor Statistics.
- By 2031, in Canada one in three will belong to a visible minority group.
  1. Toronto: nearly 63% of the population will be visible minorities. The South Asian population, which is already the largest ethnic group, could triple from 718,000 to 2.1 million.
  2. Vancouver: 59% of the population will be visible minorities, up from the current 40%.
  3. Montreal: 31% of the population will be visible minorities; Blacks and Arabs comprise most of the group.
  4. The South Asian population will be the largest ethnic group in Canada, roughly doubling from 1.3 million in 2006 to between 3.2 million and 4.1 million.

These data represent only a small amount of the growing globalization of our world.

Again, diversity means race, religion, ethnicity, age, gender, and so much more.

Our world is changing at an increasingly rapid rate. In order for businesses to thrive, they need to embrace and represent this change in their workforce and in their corporate philosophy.

Diversity works when we all recognize, understand, appreciate, and embrace each other's differences and similarities.

These include ethnic background, race, age, gender, religious faith, cultural traditions, language, sexual orientation, socio-economic background, physical abilities and disabilities, work and communication styles, as well as geographic origin and current location.

In other words, diversity includes all characteristics and experiences that define each of us as individuals.

According to a U.S. 1989 Census Bureau projection, in the next forty years (1990-2030):

- The Caucasian population will grow by 25%.
- The African-American population will increase by 68%.
- The Asian-American, Pacific Island American, and American Indian populations will increase by 70%.
- The Latino or Hispanic population in the U.S. will jump by 187%.

The population Reference Bureau has projected that, by 2080, the U.S. will be comprised of:

- 24% Latino.
- 25% African-American.
- 12% Asian-American.

This adds up to more than 50% of the white population.

Summary

Accepting that diversity is more than just a hiring policy in order to meet federal regulations is only the first step. What's really important is to have a complete understanding of what diversity means and to understand that, in order to thrive and profit in a competitive and global market, a diverse workforce is essential.

Leaders must care about embracing diversity on a personal level. Believing in the power of a diverse workforce is good.

Demonstrating that belief, adopting the philosophy in a company's mission and vision, and taking steps to communicate and follow through on this company philosophy are the next steps.

The remainder of this book is devoted to addressing those topics and helping you and your company become the powerhouse you're meant to be.

Points to Ponder:

- Ponder for a moment what diversity means to you. Would you consider your current workplace to be diverse?
- Take a look at your company's mission statement and vision. Do they incorporate a feeling of diversity and inclusion?

Notes

Chapter Two – Diversity: A Corporate Business Strategy

"The price of the democratic way of life is a growing appreciation of people's differences, not merely as tolerable, but as the essence of a rich and rewarding human experience."

-Jerome Nathanson

Thus far we've discussed the benefits of a diverse workforce and how diversity is truly defined in order to achieve these benefits. To become a thriving and competitive company that's well positioned for the future and able to quickly adapt to global changes, diversity must be embraced by a company as a whole.

The corporate vision and mission must change to adopt this new philosophy, goals must be set, and strategies must be implemented.

This chapter is devoted to talking about establishing a corporate business strategy that embraces, supports, and assesses diversity.

What Types of Strategies Need to be Developed?

Hopefully, you're at the point now where your organization is realizing that in order to thrive in the twenty-first century and to rise to the top of your industry, you must put a high value on the diversity of your employees, your clients, and even your suppliers.

Diversity must become a wholehearted and openly embraced company philosophy.

However, a philosophy is only the beginning; once a direction is chosen, strategies must be implemented to help move your company in the right direction. Goals must be set, strategies must be designed and implemented and results must be assessed.

It's also imperative that the entire company be involved in the growth and development of corporate diversity strategies.

That means education and personal evaluation is required, as not everyone understands diversity as it is defined in this book, and we're all coming from a different set of experiences, biases, and education.

Specifically, companies will want to look at their:

- Present diversity education and awareness policies and procedures.
- Current vision and mission statements.
- Recruiting strategies.
- Mentoring and training opportunities.
- Turnover rate and general employee happiness.
- Promotion policies and salaries.
- Company reputation as it relates to diversity.
- Opportunities to get involved in diversity learning opportunities (at all levels of employment).
- Ongoing assessments and employee evaluations.
- Human resources' ability to staff (need to be culturally aware).

While each organization will have its own unique approach to creating and implementing diversity strategies, there are steps to take.

These steps involve not just planning but also assessing where the company presently is, along with choosing goals and a way to evaluate success.

Let's take a look at a few of those steps:

Step One – Define what diversity means to your organization. What are your goals? What is your company vision and mission?

In this step, a company will work collectively to assess the current state of diversity, diversity initiatives, and company philosophy to evaluate what is working, what isn't working, and where to go from here.

Diversity will be incorporated into a company's vision and mission statement, and goals will be established. Employee assessments may include factors like employee satisfaction, perception of diversity and diversity initiatives, and quantifiable measurements of workforce representation. From these assessments, strategies to achieve these goals can be developed.

Step Two – Assess how your company is presently recruiting top-level talent in all areas of your company.

How do you currently recruit employees?

Is diversity taken into consideration or do hiring managers simply follow long-standing hiring practices?

What publications, organizations, and educational institutions do you recruit from?

Questions to ask include:

- What is the cultural makeup of your clients and your employees?
- Do you have employees that reflect your client base?
- Where are the gaps that need to be filled?

After assessments are conducted, determine steps to address issues and create a plan to support diversity.

For example, are you lacking diversity at the employee level? Some organizations have been able to recruit diverse employees, but their executive leadership is homogenous.

Step Three – Assess how your company is doing with retaining top-level employees.

Employee retention is a priority. Recruiting and replacing people drains company finances and reduces morale. If retention is an issue, assess why and create goals and strategies to improve retention.

Step Four – Assess present training programs.

Hiring managers are limited by their experiences and habits. In order to implement a hiring policy that embraces diversity, hiring managers must be evaluated and trained properly.

Additionally, to retain diversity, managers and supervisors must be trained for effective leadership and communication.

Step Five – Assess promotion and opportunities for growth.

Companies need to do more than simply hire a diverse workforce. Employees need to feel appreciated and recognized for their achievements. If there is a disparity here, employee morale will suffer.

It's important to put policies and procedures in place to ensure recognition at all levels for all individuals.

Step Six – Educate your employees to be aware of what diversity means and what people can do to be more aware and inclusive.

Educating your employees to be aware of their biases and stereotypes and to dialogue about them in a controlled and mutually respectful environment is essential for creating a workplace that supports and embraces diversity as it is defined in Chapter One. It's important for everyone to support one another's differences.

Step Seven – Assess your customers.

Diversity is a reality. However, whether your sales and marketing team recognizes that reality is a different story.

If you're not taking advantage of our global marketplace, you're losing money, and if you're not hiring people who are open, eager, and educated about your diverse clientele, you're losing money.

Step Eight – Assess your suppliers.

Imagine how employees would react if you only did business with one type of person. They'd recognize the hypocrisy and morale would plummet. Employee retention and productivity would suffer and profits would be affected.

Embracing suppliers who also support diversity brings your diversity mission and vision full circle. Everyone is included.

In order to become a company positioned for globalization and all the profits, innovation, and success that come along with that, you can't just say you support a diverse workplace. You have to create an atmosphere of diversity. You have to implement a business strategy that embraces diversity at all levels.

In an interview with the Mayor of Vancouver City, Gregor Robertson, we discussed the city's large multicultural population. The city of Vancouver has a strong legacy of creating diversity and embracing its multicultural city. Now the city of Vancouver is reaping the benefits of a diverse staff.

> **"Multiculturalism . . . these days it is fundamental." Mayor Gregor Robertson**

The experience of Vancouver has proven that the following strategies must be implemented to survive and thrive:

- Immigrant staff should be welcomed with open arms.
- Companies need to be respectful of employees' needs: religion, cultural function, etc.
- It is crucial to make all staff feel part of the team in order to have a sense of belonging.

He stresses that while there are some costs for employers at the beginning, it pays off at the end.

Undeniable Facts

- Statistics show that diversity affects any organization's bottom line.
- Diversity is here to stay, from blue-collar workers to professionals and business owners.
- Diversity offers an opportunity to create a business strategy with a competitive edge.
- Companies that fail to recognize and act on these opportunities will find themselves struggling, much like North American automobile companies did in the early twenty-first century.

Here are some of the key factors and considerations your company diversity strategy will want to recognize and address:

Key Factor #1
In today's global business market, management requires the expertise and tools to deal with changing demographics in the general marketplace and workforce.

Key Factor #2
Understand that the labor workforce is shifting—the bottom line is profit.

Key Factor #3
In the ever-changing global market, companies need to think globally in terms of succeeding.

Key Factor #4
It won't be easy—Canada is a nation that celebrates multiculturalism but is still having problems with it.

Key Factor #5
Racism is often more than a social dilemma—it is an economic one as well.

Key Factor #6
Diversity is part of everyday existence, at least in large cities, and visible minorities still experience racism in the workplace.

Key Factor #7
Minorities continue to come across obstacles—the obstacles are often unspoken.

Key Factor #8
While evaluating your current environment may seem like a reasonable first step, it is often quite difficult to conduct studies.

In the U.S. in 2005, Runnymede Trust carried out a study regarding ethnic minority employees. They found:

- Only 55 out of 100 companies responded to questions.
- 40% completed the questionnaire.
- 13% gave reasons such as "company is restructuring" for not completing it.
- 2% offered no response.

Key Factor #9
At the corporate level, the diversity gap is still too wide in North America.

Key Factor #10
Employees have global knowledge and converse in more than one language. This exhibits that they can think in more than one way to come up with ideas and solutions, which in the end affects the success of the company.

Key Factor #11
Embrace the diverse workforce; draw upon their unique talents, which ultimately affect your profits and productivity.

Key Factor #12

In today's market, companies are aiming at certain groups: Wal-Mart and Sears learned some time ago that what sells in one segment of the population does not sell at another location.

Staff associates who arrived from around the world possibly have better ideas on what and how to sell. These diverse staff members should be looked upon as diplomats. Utilize their talents.

When these key factors are measured, assessments and evaluations are conducted, and strategies are created to promote a more diverse workforce, change happens.

Want proof?

A national Ledger Marketing survey featuring over 1,000 Canadian companies, sponsored by Xerox Research Centre of Canada, shows that 77% of Canadian workers feel that diversity in culture and background contributes to innovation and creates a stronger business landscape. (Vancouver Sun Publication, April 5, 2008.)

Summary

The bottom line is that the competitive market is changing. In this country, the population growth of ethnic minorities and various genders, religions, ages, and sexual orientation is skyrocketing.

Internationally, we now live in a global market, and any company that wants to do business overseas must develop diverse resources in its workforce and suppliers in order to compete.

Every company, if they want to survive and thrive, must have a strategic plan for diversity.

Points To Ponder:

Business case for diversity adapted from U.S. Government Department of Personnel Hiring Documentation.

- What are the demographics of your client base?
- How many languages are spoken by your clients?
- How much does employee turnover cost your business?
- How much do you spend annually on recruitment?
- How much have discrimination suits cost your business?
- How frequently does intergroup conflict arise?
- Is there a high level of turnover within certain groups?
- Are your policies and benefits attractive to other demographic groups?
- Are you losing top employees because people don't feel valued, heard, or included?
- Do you have an internal reward system and strategy?
- Is diversity reflected in your recruitment policies and among your suppliers?
- Do you have diversity at the Board of Director, officer, and senior-management levels?
- Is diversity reflected amongst the highest salaried employees in the company?
- Is diversity reflected amongst the company's workforce as a whole?
- Do you recruit new hires in ethnic publications?
- Do you recruit at ethnic cultural or professional events?
- Do you have a membership in ethnic-American professional organizations?
- Do you make charitable contributions to ethnic organizations and support diverse volunteer initiatives?

Notes

Chapter Three – Diversity at Work: Bias-Free Staffing

"If we are to achieve a richer culture, rich in contrasting values, we must recognize the whole gamut of human potentialities, and so weave a less arbitrary social fabric, one in which each diverse human gift will find a fitting place."

-Margaret Mead

Where I live, in Vancouver, British Columbia, there was an ongoing joke. People say, if you ever get a heart attack, be in a taxi. The reason . . . an abundance of the Indian taxi drivers are heart surgeons.

Sad but true. Their credentials are not accepted and they resort to any job they can find to make a living. (I personally know an Indian psychiatrist who headed the Psychiatric Ward of a New Delhi Hospital and now works at Dairy Queen in Canada.)

Hospitals and medical facilities are missing out on a valuable resource.

Are you?

When you seek to employ and embrace a bias-free staffing policy, everyone wins. You receive highly qualified employees—the best of the best. They receive job satisfaction, a way to contribute, and a way to make the world a better place.

Generally, a diverse workforce doesn't just happen.

It has to be part of an intentional process to seek candidates from all walks of life. It goes beyond Title VII of the Civil Rights Act of 1964, which makes it illegal to discriminate against individuals on the basis of race, color, religion, sex, national origin, or disability.

A Diverse Workforce Must be Created

Before we get into the steps to embrace and institutionalize bias-free staffing, it's important to know where you and your company stand. People, leaders, and business owners often believe they work in and support diversity when the truth is typically much different. This often isn't due to anything other than the fact that when we're comfortable in our environment, we fail to notice what's really around us and we fail to notice what's missing.

Is Your Company Really Bias-Free?

Before you can begin to implement a bias-free staffing strategy, it's important to assess where your company is on the scale.

Here are a few questions to consider:

Is your company actually diverse or is it just window dressing?

Many companies consider themselves to have a diverse workforce when it just isn't the case. Racial and cultural minorities are segregated to specific types of employment. Women and senior citizens often similarly suffer from bias and stereotyping.

Does your company truly support a diverse workforce or is it just window dressing?

Are minorities represented throughout your company, at all levels and salaries?

Does your company respect and embrace diversity at all levels of the organization?

Did you know that 23% of companies have no people of color on their leadership teams? (*Boston Globe* May 19, 2009)

The same *Boston Globe* report stated that 76% of respondents said that whites and people of color advance at the same rate. And 11% had no represented diversity in their governing or leadership boards.

These statistics are representative of a common trend, and that must change for companies to prosper in coming years—globalization demands it.

According to the 2006 Census Bureau, Canada is one of the most ethnic and diverse countries in the Western world. In fact, more than 5 million people belong to a visible minority—that represents 16.2% of the population. The South Asian community, is expected to be the third largest ethnic community in Canada, after the British and French.

However, despite this broad cultural representation, visible minorities comprise only 5.2% of senior management in Canadian companies and 1.5% of executive management in the public sector.

Do you understand everything that encompasses diversity?

In recent years, efforts have been made to bring people of color into organizations—but often they face restrictions climbing the corporate ladder.

A study done by Professor Phillip Oreopoulos at the University of British Columbia and reported on by CBC News revealed that people with English-sounding names had a 40% greater chance of finding employment than those with non-English names. In this study, 6,000 mock résumés were sent in Toronto with English names, and then were sent again with ethnic names such as Chu and Singh.

The result . . . English names received 40% more call backs for an interview than Indian, Pakistani, or Chinese names, even though the résumés had the same qualifications, including a BA plus six years of training.

A similar study was conducted in the U.S., in both Boston and Chicago, and found similar results. White-sounding names were 50% more likely to be called back for blue-collar jobs than African-American names.

While this may or may not surprise you, it should give us pause. We often say we support diversity but our underlying processes, biases, and awareness result in the opposite behavior. We end up discriminating against minorities, forming and supporting stereotypes, and avoiding people who are different from us.

Often such biases are due to historical, cultural, and social factors. They're learned, but that's not an excuse; it's merely the foundation for an honest dialogue.

Despite Canada's boasts about diversity, survey results tell a different story. Résumés were tailored to job requirements and sent to 2,000 online jobs postings to employers across twenty different categories.

About 16% of English names received a call back compared to 11% of ethnic names with the same level of education. Call-back rates dropped to 8% for ethnic names whose education was outside Canada. This study shows that an applicant's name could mean a lot more than their qualifications.

Would the same thing happen in your organization? If you received two résumés, one with an English name and one with an Indian, Chinese, or other ethnic name, both with equal education and backgrounds, which person would get called in for an interview?

Are your present employees happy with your diversity progression?

In a study conducted by Commonwealth Compact, 88% of 111 organizations surveyed stated that diversity has improved during the last five years. Some of the companies who participated were Wal-Mart, Staples, and various healthcare and nonprofit organizations with 180,000 or more employees.

In the same study, 42% of the organizations reported they were not happy with diversity progression.

Does your corporation pay an equal salary to all groups? Or is there some disparity?

In 2004, the Canadian study conducted by the Conference Board showed there is a huge wage gap—14.5%—between ethnic populations and the rest of Canadians. The gap is persistent and deepening. One of the reasons for this widening gap is the continual failure to recognize foreign credentials. In addition, many non-Canadian residents do not have Canadian work experiences. Narrowing wage gaps will not only benefit people of color but also the rest of the Canadian economy.

Is your corporation taking steps to embrace diversity and all of the powerful benefits that go along with it?

Some companies, such as KMPG, are discovering that promoting visible minorities gives them an edge in competition. Makes good business sense, right?

A wealth of evidence suggests that companies with diverse leadership, both in management and on the board, outperform companies without. Despite this evidence, many Canadian companies have been slow to diversify because they need more hardcore evidence.

Education is required on all levels to bring about an awareness of what diversity means and how a company benefits from bias-free staffing and a diverse workforce.

How Do You Go About Employing a Diverse Workforce? What Exactly is Bias-Free Staffing?

In this section, we'll take a look at some of the steps required to begin building a diverse workforce.

Again, the benefits of a diverse workforce are limitless. They include happier and more productive employees, less employee turnover, innovation, a better ability to meet the needs of your growing global client base, a better ability to target prospects all around the world, and a better corporate image, which all lead to attracting the cream-of-the-crop applicants from all walks of life.

Step One - Preparing the Search

Your search begins with your recruiting and hiring staff. If the people on your staff who are assigned to recruit and hire have biases or stereotypes, or are not in line with your corporate philosophy, then steps need to be taken to rectify this. Education, training, and regular assessments are great ways to ensure your search starts off on the right food.

Make sure to:

- Establish and review hiring policies and procedures.
- Make sure your hiring staff, policies, and procedures are culturally competent—meaning they are aware of, understand, and support the company's diversity goals.
- Outline and draft your necessary requirements for each job. Make sure this definition is approved of and understood by all.
- Review present workforce demographics and create a strategy to employ a diverse workforce. (Note: you cannot intentionally seek to add a specific type of person to your workforce and must always hire based on credentials and best fit; however, if you are looking to add diversity to your workforce, then strategies like placing ads in ethnic publications, for example, may be a good way to reach out. We'll talk more about recruiting methods in just a bit.)

Step Two – Create policies and procedures to assist your staffing department in "casting a wide net" when recruiting for vacant positions:

- Advertise the position in a variety of local publications, including publications aimed at myriad cultures and communities.
- Encourage employment staff to network in their communities. This brings about the need to have the people recruiting for and staffing your company come from diverse backgrounds.
- Attend a variety of professional conferences geared toward a variety of minorities. For example, there are job fairs for senior citizens, women's professional organizations and events, and multicultural events.
- Use recruiters who pool from a wide resource of applicants.
- Take steps before, during, and after the search as part of an ongoing strategy to employ a diverse workforce and to improve your company's reputation as one that supports diversity at all levels of the company.

This is, of course, an ongoing strategy and one that begins with your next new hire. The better your company's reputation as one that supports diversity, the better candidates you'll receive.

Step Three – Applicant Screening Process

Once the applications begin coming in, policies and procedures should have been established to identify qualified candidates without allowing any bias to enter into the decision.

Earlier we cited several studies where people who are assumed to be Caucasian or have English-sounding names received more call backs and job offers than equally qualified non-English or non-white names.

This is a bias that must not be allowed to enter into the applicant screening process. Qualifications and requirements have been defined, in step one, and any candidate who meets these requirements should make it through the first level of screening.

Step Four - Evaluating and Communicating with the Applicant Pool

Once you've undergone the first level of screening, usually from the résumé and cover letter, the next step is to communicate with your applicants. This is typically done with a telephone call or a phone interview. This is a great way to further screen a candidate but also leaves room for discrimination, bias, and stereotypes.

The person(s) conducting the phone interviews must be trained and evaluated on their ability to make an unbiased hiring decision. Each applicant should be asked the same questions, with the interviewer careful to steer clear of unlawful inquiries.

In an effort to eliminate any intended or unintended bias when recording the results of the interview, consider actually making an audio recording of each interview. This way the entire hiring committee can make an assessment on the qualifications of the candidates. (It should be noted that it's important to gain the applicant's permission to record the interview.)

Of course, the next phase is to determine which candidates will be brought in for face-to-face interviews. When scheduling interviews, it's important to agree on a process ahead of time and to remain consistent with each and every candidate. Before the interview:

Determine who is going to meet with the candidate, in what order people will meet with the candidate, and how long they'll meet with the candidate.

Develop a group of core questions based on the position's job requirements and make sure each candidate is asked the same questions. Make sure questions are focused on discovering what the candidate potentially brings to the position.

Questions you should focus on:

- Specific requirements for the position.
- Skills and education required for the position.
- Demonstrated experience or ability to perform required tasks.
- An ability to enhance your present workforce.
- An ability and willingness to work in a diverse environment and to uphold corporate philosophies.

Finally, reference checks should be conducted and all necessary testing performed. Again, this process should be outlined and approved before any candidates are ever contacted and each candidate's references should receive the same questions and treatment.

Applicants—all applicants, including those contacted by phone—should be contacted regarding the status of the position.

Now it's time to extend the offer.

Step Five - Making the Offer

When it comes to hiring, this is the point we're all waiting for—making the offer and the potential negotiations required to obtain your chosen candidate.

This step, like the prior steps, should follow a preplanned and documented approach. And salaries should be determined when the job description is drafted and approved, not after the candidate has been met and it's determined that they would accept a much smaller salary.

Remember, people learn quite quickly how their salary ranks when compared to others in the company and any bias, whether intentional or unintentional, can be perceived as discrimination and foster an unhappy workforce.

It should also be noted that as part of an optimal hiring strategy, all records of your search should be retained. It helps should any issues come up, and it's a great resource for the next open position.

Summary

We didn't get into government equal employment policies and procedures, which often stipulate what you can and cannot ask prospective employees, because that's not what this book or our philosophy is about. Rather, when you're striving to embrace and benefit from a diverse workforce, equal employment policies should be obvious. The goal should be instead to find the most qualified candidate from a diverse pool of applicants.

Thus recruiting is the very first and, often times, the most important step in employing bias-free staffing. If you're pooling applicants from every walk of life, you're going to receive a diverse pool of applicants. The better your company reputation, the better quality candidates you'll receive.

In this chapter we've outlined the following hiring steps, including:

- Cultivating a positive perception of your company.
- Educating and preparing your hiring and recruiting staff.
- Recruitment of a diverse applicant pool.
- Actual hire.

What's next? Leading your new diverse workforce into the twenty-first century and beyond!

Points to Ponder:

- Your company should be prepared to reflect diversity in all work categories and at all salary levels.
- Recruitment must be advertised in ethnic publications in addition to mainstream ones.
- Biases towards people of color still exist, although it may not be as prominent as it was in the past. (*Business Week* October 7, 2009)
- Corporate America continues to have troubles when it comes to diversity. Large numbers of publicly traded businesses are often headed by white males.
- In America's largest 100 corporations, African-Americans occupy only 9% of board positions, yet they represent almost 13% of the population and 12% of the labor workforce.
- Women and minorities represented only 14.8% of the top 500 board seats in 2007. That's the same as it was in 2005, according to Catalyst Inc. (Report on Business May 23, 2009)
- Despite Canada's large ethnic population, that same diversity isn't reflected in the boardroom.
- Visible minorities make up 5.2% of senior management in large Canadian companies and only 1.6% of executive management in the public sector.
- The situation has deteriorated from 2005; recent immigrant men earned only 63 cents on the dollar compared to Canadian-born men, down from 85 cents in 1980.
- Promoting diversity makes good sense because there is a larger pool to choose from. It generates international clients, as well.
- Studies have been done that show companies that have diverse leadership in management and on their board have outperformed organizations without diverse leadership. (Peanut, Boston Consulting)

Notes

Chapter Four – Successfully Leading a Diverse Workforce

"Leaders provide the visibility and commit the time and resources to make diversity happen – it's a top priority and personal responsibility."

-The U.S. Dept. of Commerce Best Practices in Achieving Workforce Diversity

Without leadership, diversity cannot happen.

Goals can be defined, initiatives implemented, and strategies outlined from here to kingdom come, but if leadership isn't 100% behind the programs, diversity won't happen.

Why?

Because leaders provide the visibility and commit the time and resources to make diversity happen—it's a top priority and personal responsibility.

Leaders—effective leaders—are aware of what it takes to make diversity happen. They embrace communication and recognize their own limitations. They promote training and educate, mentor, recruit, train, and monitor the progress of diversity initiatives.

They have their finger on the pulse of the workforce, client base, and suppliers.

Leaders are also aware of the potential obstacles to achieving diversity.

Hundreds and thousands of people relocate every week around the world. For instance, in Canada alone since 1990, more than 2 million newcomers from all over the globe have settled in the country.

It is estimated that the visible minority population in Canada is 17% of the total population, with almost 70% of new immigrants coming from Asia and the rest from the Third World.

In the past, the North American workplace was quite homogeneous. Workers for the most part knew the unwritten rules about what was expected and how things were done. Today's workforce, however, includes employees from various backgrounds who bring with them different workplace perspectives, preferences, and expectations. The rules can no longer remain unwritten.

Managers may find articulating the rules to be challenging, but the benefits will be considerable.

Managers must set the example for their employees. They will need to create an inclusive environment in which all employees understand, value, and respect each other's differences.

What Today's Workforce Looks Like

Take a look around you and you'll see a very different picture than what our parents saw on the job. Of course, many of us are working side by side with people who are the same age as our parents.

It's an amazing time!
Currently there are five different groups working side by side:

1. Most experienced – born before 1946.
2. Baby Boomers – born between 1946 and 1964.
3. Gen X – born between 1966 and 1977.
4. Millennials - reaching adulthood around the turn of the century.
5. In addition, a multicultural diverse workforce (gay, lesbian, and a variety of ethnicities).

What Managers Can Do to Embrace, Support, and Lead a Diverse Workforce

Managers are the leaders of a business. They're the ones who set the bar and then follow up by walking the talk, so to speak. If a company wants its workforce to be diverse and to support and embrace diversity, then it too has to support and embrace diversity.

It's about being a good role model, about creating not only strategies, policies, and procedures to support diversity, but also providing training, mentoring, and support for everyone.

This chapter is devoted to showing not only why it's important for managers to step up and recognize the importance of a diverse workforce, it's also about getting the gears spinning and brainstorming ideas to create goals and initiate strategies to lead your company and workforce into the twenty-first century.

Here are just a few ideas to get those creative juices flowing:

Begin by assessing your personal beliefs about diversity.

It's difficult to lead others when you're unsure of your direction, beliefs, values, and potential biases and stereotypes. This isn't a judgement, but rather a time to be honest with yourself. We all have preconceptions about a variety of things. We grew up with them but that doesn't make them true.

In order to become aware of others, create self-awareness (dislikes, likes, prejudices, etc.) of yourself. Determine what you believe to be true and ask yourself if it really is true.

Self-management.

It's also important to know what peeves and idiosyncrasies you have and how they affect your ability to manage, lead, and communicate. Again, this isn't about judgment; we all have strengths and weaknesses. Acknowledge yours and assess how they have an impact on your ability to manage and lead. Know what pushes your hot buttons and learn how to avoid having them pushed!

(A quick way to ensure a positive reaction is to listen carefully and pause two seconds before responding. It helps eliminate any negative reactions or overreactions.)

Sharpen social skills to be able to accommodate others.

I'm sure you know that we each have our own personality style.

And there are various experts and analysis tools to establish and define your communication style. Common types/definitions include:

- Expresser.
- Driver.
- Relater.
- Analyzer.

Learn your personal communication style and learn how to interact with other communication styles.

Embrace empathy.

Empathy is defined as the ability to identify with and understand another's situation, feelings, and motives. When you can embrace and feel empathy, it puts you in the shoes of the person and together you can reach your goals.

Learn the ability to quickly assess people's weak and strong points.

Why? Well, it's a great tool when negotiating, and often when you're working towards a mutually beneficial solution within your team of employees, that's exactly what you're doing.

You're trying to make everyone happy, and being able to quickly assess someone's strengths and weaknesses will not only help you negotiate, it'll help you build powerful teams and interoffice committees. You can group people together who complement each other.

Build trust with staff.

Trust building is an ongoing process and not something that happens overnight. It's accomplished by saying what you mean, by showing compassion and trust in your workforce, by showing appreciation, and by being able to deliver constructive criticism. Additionally, trust is earned by following through on what you promise.

Be able to inspire.

There's little that's more inspiring than finding a leader who has strong convictions you believe in and can grasp onto, and who takes steps to follow through on those convictions. When you can be that person, the one who expresses their convictions and who takes distinct steps to make things happen, that's the beginning of being an inspirational leader.

Other steps include being someone employees can trust, someone who isn't afraid to make difficult decisions, someone who provides opportunity and hope, and also someone who honestly enjoys their job and their life.

Make them part of the team.

Teamwork is an exciting way to work. It fosters creativity and enthusiasm and it gives each person a role to fill. It also tells your employees they're valued and you trust them—key ingredients for employee satisfaction.

Trust and respect them.

It seems everyone has a horror story about a micromanager. It's just not a good way to build a positive working relationship and it belittles your role as a manager. An effective leader defines and assigns tasks, creates a system of assessment and evaluation, and then trusts employees have the ability to make it happen.

Encourage feedback.

Feedback is a two-way street and, while a manager may be great at providing feedback, they often forget to ask for it. Now we're not suggesting you ask your staff to critique you, but rather provide feedback on ongoing projects, diversity initiatives, and so on.

Your staff has valuable insight and information; take advantage of that and you'll do more than create a positive relationship with them and a positive work environment. You'll also grow the business.

Bring out the best talent from a diverse workforce.

One of the benefits of a diverse workforce is the power behind all of the experiences and ideas your team has. However, if that insight and creativity is never accessed, you're missing out on an extremely valuable asset. To successfully manage a diverse workforce, initiatives need to be put into place to encourage expression, assess skills and strengths, and utilize each employee in their optimal position within the company.

Understand that cultural differences could lead to miscommunication.

For example, looking straight in the eyes of a South Asian person could be disrespectful. When you're speaking, they might look down: a sign of respect. In Western cultures, we may view it as lying or not paying attention.

As a manager and change leader, it's your responsibility to educate yourself first and foremost and then to pass that education on to your staff.

Maintaining Employee Faith in Diversity Initiatives

It's one thing to say you support a diverse workforce and another thing to actually create, lead, and manage diversity initiatives. When employees lose faith in the company's diversity commitment, they lose faith in the company.

When this happens, companies lose productivity, lose profits, and lose employees.

This can happen by:

- Promoting staff in name only, not wages or duties.
- Not compensating employees for their efforts.
- Not implementing mentoring and ongoing training for new employees.
- Approaching diversity as a series of unlinked schemes. It takes cooperation from the entire organization—managers and staff—to embrace and sustain a diverse workforce.

However, leaders can build and maintain faith by:

- Making sure to design clear diversity initiatives and objectives.
- Creating methods to monitor the changes and make improvements on a regular basis.
- Always clarifying the rationale for benefits, challenges, and the importance of multiculturalism in the place of work.
- Incorporating new strategies to bring about different cultural work styles.
- Improving the cross-cultural communications skills.
- Implementing a bias-free hiring procedure including staffing and recruitment.
- Removing employment barriers.
- Creating a comprehensive and positive working environment.
- Making certain that all employees are made part of company policy and that their involvement actually matters to the success of the company.
- Creating an overall strategy and avoiding an intermittent approach. Many corporations allocate resources but long-term strategy is rarely thought out. Try not to leave gaps.
- Making diversity a business strategy—connecting community, education, and community investment. Diversity should be viewed as achieving long-term business goals. It's important to think of productivity, safety, quality, and employee fulfillment.
- Creating short and long-term goals—these programs must be updated.

- Having measures in place to track progress every four to six months.
- Implementing a communication plan. On many occasions, diversity is something that very few know about, except the people of color. Get every person involved.
- Appointing a diversity team.
- Letting the employees know that diversity and inclusion will make their jobs more stimulating and they will gain knowledge of new things that they were unaware of before.

Managers Have to Juggle Many Balls

In addition to facing their own biases, implementing diversity initiatives, evaluating, measuring, and recognizing, managers and leaders face a variety of challenges. It's not an easy job but the payoff, both professionally and personally, is well worth it.

Differences in cultural values demand an extra set of skills when trying to motivate changes in diverse workforces, unlike with workers from similar backgrounds.

Here are three methods:

1. **Interpretation**: Understand why an objectionable attitude is taking place.
   For example, when workers communicate in their native language, some supervisors may think they are saying something against them or the company. The fact is that they may feel they can articulate more efficiently to get the job done.

2. **Expectations**: It is essential to make clear the expectations in a simple language. In many cases expectations in their native land might be carried out in different methods.
   Many new immigrants hardly ever express their views or oppositions to the management. They do not want to be looked

down on as complainers. Many newcomers have a great deal of admiration for management and the company.

3. **Affirmative Reinforcement**: It is very important to give constructive feedback when due. Try to distance yourself whenever a problem arises. Take a moment to assess the situation and then clearly offer suggestions to solve the problem.

So now that the wheels are spinning and ideas for being a diversity leader are coming forth, it's important to see how these ideas will fit into an overall strategy to retain and lead a diverse workforce. We've broken it down into steps to take.

These steps include:

#1 Commitment
#2 Assessment and Evaluation
#3 Training and Education
#4 Creating a Supportive Work Environment
#5 Sustaining Commitment

As you can see, the previous questions and thoughts on how to lead a diverse workforce tie directly into these five essential steps.

Let's explore each step individually.

Step One - Obtaining Commitment from Managers and Company Leaders

Without commitment from company leaders and managers, diversity initiatives will fall flat.

Leaders and managers must be on board and held accountable for creating an environment that includes everyone and understands the value of diversity.

Leaders must also be ready, willing, and able to:

- Assign adequate resources to their diversity goals and objectives.
- Be actively involved in creating diversity initiatives and goals.
- Be actively involved in assessing and evaluating success.
- Be held accountable for successes and failures.

Step Two – Assessing and Evaluating Your Current Workplace Environment

Before goals can be set and initiatives implemented, it's important for leaders and managers to have a realistic assessment of the current workplace environment. This means knowing:

- What structures are in place to support diversity management?
- What challenges or obstacles need to be overcome?
- How is diversity presently incorporated into the company's vision or mission statement?
- What diversity training is presently available and how is it working?
- What formal or informal mentoring program is in place and how is it working?
- What diversity awards and incentives are in place right now and are they working and being followed through on?
- How do employees presently feel about the company's diversity philosophy and initiatives?

Step Three – Training and Education

Training and education are a continuous process. With many companies, training and education is a necessity after a sexual-harassment suit or a discrimination suit.

They're a reaction rather than a standing policy of diversity and acceptance. This is a costly, detrimental, and backwards way to conduct business.

However, smart managers and leaders understand the value of honest discussion, training, and education as part of a corporate policy.

They also regularly assess employee strengths and weaknesses, provide training and education to fill in the gaps, and recruit employees to complement and further establish a supportive workforce.

DiversityInc's Diversity-Training Tips:

- Make training mandatory for the entire workforce, not just managers. If it isn't, those who really need it won't attend.

- Hold the training frequently so there are no excuses for not attending, and make certain it lasts a full day.

- Training can't exist in a vacuum. Make sure there are sufficient metrics and follow-ups.

Step Four – Creating a Supportive Work Environment

A supportive workforce means:
- Providing a flexible and supportive work environment.
- An emphasis on learning and development.
- Implementing effective rewards and recognition systems.
- Ensuring supervisors and managers are provided leadership and diversity training. Their understanding of the benefits and rewards of a diverse workforce helps create a supportive work environment that enhances the potential of all employees.
- Implementing and supporting quality-of-work/life programs like:
  o Alternative work schedules.
  o Family leave programs.

- o Part-time employment and job sharing.
- o Telecommuting.
- o Time off for religious holidays (regardless of the religion).
- o Dependent care support programs.
- o Employee assistance programs.

- Supporting job applicants with disabilities.
- Ensuring that all receive a safe and productive work environment.
- Supporting community spirit and a sense of belonging.

> "The mark of a truly successful diversity program is one that becomes ingrained in the culture and the business processes of an agency and is sustained over time."
>
> - U.S. Office of Personnel Management

Step Five – Sustaining the Commitment

Sustainability as it relates to a diverse workforce can be accomplished by:

- Monitoring results.
- Holding people at all levels accountable.
- Celebrating success.
- Continuing to set new diversity goals and implementing strategies to achieve them.

Summary

Managers have a decidedly difficult and important role to play in the changes ahead. They must be the leaders while at the same time they have their own biases, stereotypes, preconceptions, and needs to balance.

Managers are in a position to change the face of their corporation, to position the company for tremendous growth, create a competitive advantage, and provide the potential for global profits.

Beyond that, hopefully there is the personal satisfaction of being instrumental to having your workforce represent the multicultural variety growing each and every day. So what's next?

Retaining that amazing and diverse staff!

Points to Ponder:

How Diversity Impacts Modern Business And How Managers Can Adapt.

- Demographics are clearly changing: ethnicity, religion, sexual orientation, age, various skills and disabilities, levels of education, and languages are more vital than ever before.
- Customer needs have changed; expectations of services offered are extremely high. Employers must be aware of these new and demanding attitudes.
- Serve customers in other languages—many companies offer services in languages other than English: Cantonese, Mandarin, Spanish, Hindi, or Punjabi.
- Consider learning another language—Cantonese, Hindi, or Spanish—to stay competitive in the twenty-first century. In many other countries, it is the norm for people to know more than one language.
- Technology is continuously evolving and customers and staff must remain current.
- Understanding of competitors, merchandise, and emerging markets is essential.
- Organizations must adapt to the changes to be successful.
- It is vital to have a steady workforce; otherwise, it becomes a rotating door.
- Create a work atmosphere that is enjoyable and stable.
- Open communication channels between management and employees are essential, especially regarding goals and objectives.
- It is important to manage, retain, develop, and focus. Evaluate progress.
- Produce a diversity memo and assign a diversity spokesperson—keep employees at all levels involved in the development.

- In the role of a diversity spokesperson, accountability and responsibility are very important.
- Managers need to know what is in it for them (e.g., profits).
- Effective communication is the key in leading a diverse workforce.

Notes

Chapter Five – Retaining a Multicultural Staff

"We all should know that diversity makes for a rich tapestry and we must understand that all the threads of the tapestry are equal in value no matter what their color."

-Maya Angelou

We hinted at assessment, training, and mentoring as steps to leading a diverse workforce; they're also essential for retaining a multicultural staff.

Employees' views and involvement are key to the success of diversity initiatives, and organizations must view employee participation as a necessary part of a diversity philosophy in order to develop a welcoming, thriving, and diverse workforce.

Leaders of the best organizations understand they must support their employees in learning how to effectively interact with others. They recognize they should encourage employees to continue to learn new communication, technical, and management skills.

Finally, they recognize the impact that diverse clients will have upon the success or failure of an organization and the inherent benefit of having a diverse workforce to understand and meet these needs.

In this chapter, we'll take a look at the benefits of retaining a multicultural staff, how to retain a multicultural staff, and a few specific ideas to take to get it done.

Benefits of Retaining a Multicultural Staff

The benefits, as we've mentioned, of retaining a diverse workforce are limitless.

- Companies achieve a higher retention rate, meaning they don't have to spend as much of their budget on hiring and training new employees.
- Employee morale remains higher because retention strategies typically embrace tools like mentoring, recognition, and creating a supportive and welcoming workplace.
- Employees are more productive, they're more responsive, and profits increase.

Studies have shown that mentoring offers significant benefits to retaining employees. A University of Pennsylvania study of more than 1,000 employees found that those who participated in mentoring programs were promoted at six times the rate of those who were not involved in mentoring programs, and the retention rate for those in the program was 72% versus the 49% retention rate for non-members.

The National Black MBA Association surveyed 2,875 members and found that they valued mentoring almost twice as much as they valued performance feedback.

Additionally, there are a number of benefits to specifically focusing on retaining employees from diverse backgrounds.

For example:

1. Employees who feel comfortable as themselves will be more productive.
2. Studies have revealed that new immigrants are likely to be more loyal than native-born.
3. Employees who are comfortable as themselves and feel accepted and appreciated will actually go out of their way to accommodate management. However, once they've been disillusioned, they will never forget their experiences and will eventually move on.
4. Various studies have been conducted where people from diverse backgrounds in one setting with the right skills and abilities can produce higher-quality solutions.

How to Retain a Diverse Staff

To retain a multicultural staff, here are just a few items to consider:

1. All employees must be treated equally and with respect.

2. The working environment must be conducive to development, communication, and growth.
3. Establish a secure and friendly environment—no staff member should feel a bias against them.
4. All employees should be made to feel welcome, respected, and treasured.
5. Management should accommodate for special occasions. For example, among many ethnic communities there are obligations to extended family members that are not the norm in the Western world: birthdays, funerals, weddings, hospital visits, religious functions, and daily prayers are just a few examples.
6. The labor atmosphere has to be friendly—have a business culture in place where they can be "complete" and be who they are. This means accommodating their religion, their dress, or simply their packing ethnic food for lunch.
7. The management organization must be totally aware of the skills and talents of their diverse workforce; this is carried out by making them comfortable, valued, and having the same goals to conquer.
8. All employees are offered the same opportunity in climbing the corporate ladder.

These objectives are attained by three basic strategies: training and education, creating a welcoming workplace, and mentoring.

Mentoring as an Initiative to Retain a Multicultural Staff

There are essentially two types of mentoring programs: formal and informal.

Formal Mentoring

Formal programs include new-hire programs where each new hire is assigned a peer mentor. The peer mentor's responsibility is to help explain the job and to facilitate social mentoring to help the new hire adjust and learn the ropes, so to speak.

Other formal programs can include mentoring programs designed to help employees fast-track themselves to leadership positions while focusing on long-term career development.

Informal Mentoring

Informal mentoring, on the other hand, is typically facilitated by forming groups. For example, networking groups or smaller group mentoring programs function well as informal mentoring situations.

It's important to note that it's not an either/or type of situation; companies can and do have both formal and informal mentoring programs to help with employee retention and satisfaction.

The key to either type of mentoring program is to make mentoring cross-cultural. This means establishing policies and procedures, or offering incentives if it's an informal mentoring group, to include people from all walks of life, including their own.

Additionally, like all diversity strategies and employment retention strategies, it's important to create quantifiable goals, to measure these goals, and to assess the success or failure.

This can be accomplished by measuring employee retention and comparing it to retention before mentoring programs have been established. You can also measure more finite data like new-hire retention, promotion, and employee satisfaction.

Finally, it's important to stand on the metaphorical rooftop and announce success. When other employees realize the benefits of employee retention programs they'll more likely participate; it'll contribute to their faith in the company and to the overall company reputation, which of course helps you find those high-quality employees and makes building a diverse workforce easier.

Retaining Staff through Training and Education

Training and education, as it relates to retaining a diverse workforce, has two paths to take. On the one hand you very much want to provide opportunities for career development.

This helps you keep employees engaged and focused on their success, and the company reaps the benefits.

For example, companies that offer language learning programs, seminars on marketing and the new global market, and opportunities to understand and utilize new technologies stay ahead of the game competitively. They also have a higher retention rate because employees recognize the value of learning opportunities.

- Customer awareness has changed based on globalization and the expectations are very high. Employers must be aware of these attitudes. Serve customers in other languages—many companies offer services in languages other than English, such as Cantonese, Mandarin, Spanish, Hindi, or Punjabi.
- Technology is always evolving and customers and staff must stay current.
- Knowledge of competitors, products, and emerging markets is essential.
- Organizations must adapt to the changes to be successful.

The second path that training and education must follow in order to retain a diverse workforce is to provide a continual dialogue and education on diversity.

This includes:

- Honest personal assessments of biases, attitudes and beliefs.
- Honest dialogue.
- Established goals to achieve as they relate to diversity and understanding as well as embracing and working with differences.
- Teaching verbal communication skills that make everyone feel appreciated and respected.
- Teaching listening, compassion, and appreciation skills that make everyone feel respected.

Training and education is an ongoing and continuous process that must be embraced as part of the company philosophy. That means it must be provided to all levels of employees, from the top senior executives to the lower-tier employees.

Training must also recognize that people have different learning styles to reach all employees optimally and make everyone feel included and respected.

Finally, the other important facet to retaining a multicultural workforce is to provide a welcoming atmosphere.

Creating an Environment Where Everyone Belongs

It is very important to have a stable workforce; otherwise, your company becomes a revolving door. Constantly having to replace employees is costly both in time and money and it has a detrimental effect on company morale.

To create a welcoming atmosphere designed to achieve a high level of employee retention, the two keys we discussed earlier are most certainly part of that equation. Mentoring and diversity training and education both go a long way toward creating an environment where people feel welcome.

On the surface, this may seem like an easy task; however, a quick employee assessment on how welcoming your workplace is might tell a different story.

While there is no right way to achieve this ideal environment, the best approach is to get your employees involved in creating strategies and establishing initiatives to improve workforce morale.

Nicola Webb, General Manager, Human Resources Services with city of Surrey, British Columbia, offers the following suggestions for companies:

- Try to be flexible. Certain cultures have different requests such as attending funerals/weddings of extended relatives/ friends, which is often not the norm among the mainstream Canadians.
- Be very proactive by celebrating/acknowledging special occasions such as Diwali (Indian festival of lights), Vaisakhi (Sikh New Year), Chinese New Year, Ramadan, etc. The occasions are cherished and embraced.

Create a team of employees from all levels of the company whose directive is to improve the atmosphere and ensure all employees feel welcome and respected. This may include appreciation days, welcoming committees, and recognition for accomplishments as they relate to diversity goals.

This, coupled with mentoring, training and education, and leaders who walk the talk and model appropriate behavior, sets the stage for a high level of employee satisfaction and employee retention.

In the book Generations at Work, by Ron Zemke, Claire Raines and Bob Filipczak, they provide the following acronym, ACORN, to outline how to create a welcoming atmosphere.

A – Accommodate employee differences

C – Create workplace choices

O – Operate from a sophisticated management style

R – Respect competence and initiative

N – Nourish retention

While it's important to point out that the book's focus is on managing the generation clash where there are Veterans and Generation-X people working together side by side, each with their own language and ways of doing things, the points are still valid for diversity as it is defined in Chapter One.

To create a workforce that welcomes all employees from all walks of life and makes them feel respected and valued, differences must be accommodated for, choices must be made available without judgment, management must embrace diversity personally and professionally, and respect must be given—these are the keys to employee retention.

Summary

Employee retention isn't just good for employee morale—it's good for business.

Better employee retention provides a better company image with the public. This means it's easier to recruit top-level talent. If no one ever leaves, it's a great sign to a potential employee.

Better employee retention also provides a better company image with your clients and suppliers. It's easier to develop long-term relationships with people, and that means profits.

Better employee retention initiatives also provide more productive and happier employees. When people are happy to come to work, they work better.

Better employee retention means less turnover and fewer resources dedicated to recruiting.

Bottom line: Better Employee Retention = Profits

Points to Ponder:

- What is the present state of your employee satisfaction?
- Do you have mentoring programs, either formal or informal?
- Is training and education a priority?
- Is diversity training and education required and consistently provided?
- What does your company do to embrace cultural events and celebrations?
- What does your company do to make your workplace somewhere that everyone feels welcome and respected?

Notes

Chapter Six – Avoiding Stereotypes

"Difference is of the essence of humanity. Difference is an accident of birth and it should therefore never be the source of hatred or conflict. The answer to difference is to respect it. Therein lies a most fundamental principle of peace: respect for diversity."

-John Hume

Whether it's a blonde joke, a lawyer joke, or a Polish joke, the truth is we all have stereotypes about certain groups of people. We've grown up with them; we've heard them in our homes, on television, at the water cooler, and when we're hanging out with our friends and family. Stereotypes permeate our lives and our cultures.

Unfortunately, these very same stereotypes, which we find occasionally humorous and generally harmless, are the opposite of funny.

They're quite harmful and limiting not only to those we stereotype but also to ourselves. And trust me on this one, stereotypes apply to everyone and chances are you personally fall into several stereotypes.

The goal of this chapter is to help people of all levels and from all walks of life understand how we form stereotypes, how they limit us, and how to overcome them. We'll also address what companies can do to avoid stereotypes for more productivity, profits and a better workplace environment.

The Various Kinds of Stereotypes

There are too many stereotypes to fit into this book. They encompass every race, religion, gender, and sexual orientation. They even cover hair color. I'm sure you've heard it said that redheaded women are fiery and blondes are dumb.

There are also regional stereotypes. In the U.S., people from the South are sometimes depicted as dimwitted hillbillies or racists, and people from the West Coast depicted as shallow and materialistic.

What are some other stereotypes you're familiar with? What about the stereotype that Asians are often perceived as hard and effective workers, but are not outgoing.

South Asians could be native born, but often are viewed as outsiders.

African-Americans are looked upon as not being hard workers. It is not their culture but rather their skin color that holds them back from succeeding in the workplace. This has been demonstrated in a study conducted by Catalyst, an international organization.

None of these stereotypes are positive or productive.

How do You Define a Stereotype?

One definition of a stereotype is a bias, an inflexible belief about a particular group.

Another definition, provided by Stedman Graham in his book *Diversity Leaders not Labels*, suggests a stereotype might be an exaggerated image or distorted truth about a person or group, allowing for little or no social variation or individual difference, usually passed along by peers, family members, or the media.

Unfortunately, because stereotypes are so deeply embedded, they're often difficult to remove, even if we want to. Studies have shown that no matter how devoted we are to diversity and an open-minded and even approach to all, we still subconsciously hold onto negative beliefs and labels for people. These hidden beliefs affect our actions and reactions.

However, all is not lost. New experiences, honest assessment, and dialogue can change and eliminate stereotypes.

Where do Stereotypes Come From?

Essentially, we're all guilty of forming stereotypes about others. They come to us from the media, from family members, from our peers, and from our personal experiences.

All cultures are guilty of stereotyping: Indians have preconceived perceptions about the Chinese, Chinese have preconceived perceptions about the African-Americans, etc.

As humans we tend to label people because it makes us feel safe and superior, and because it's often easier than looking at people too deeply.

In the past, most people did not travel internationally and often lived in the same neighborhood most of their lives. They probably stayed away from people who were different from them. But today that is not the case because the world is becoming more global and people from various places around the world are relocating.

Somehow, we need to embrace and understand these people who look different, dress differently, eat different kinds of food, and have mannerisms that are different. People often form prejudices simply because it is easier than doing the work to get to know a person. Processing information takes time and effort. Stereotyping does not.

It's easy to be tricked by our senses to be judgmental about those who are different from us. But if we do, we run the risk of forming conclusions that are erroneous and mutually detrimental.

To make peace with the reality of diversity, we need to take the time and make the effort to understand and embrace people who are different from us.

How Stereotypes Hurt Us

In the corporate world, there's a high price to pay for stereotypes.

- Litigation.
- Lost employees.
- Poor employee morale.

- Lost sales and lost customers.
- Difficulty hiring top-level employees.
- Difficulty retaining employees.
- Diminished productivity.

However, we also suffer personal consequences when we judge people based on biases, labels, and stereotypes. We miss out on valuable experiences, insights, and amazing relationships. We also miss out on connecting with others on a genuine level.

Breaking Down Stereotypes

Breaking down, recognizing, and eliminating stereotypes begins with dialogue. Conversation reduces bias because we learn more about each other and reach understanding. Conversation reduces and limits the spread of bias by educating us on misinformation.

Imagine, if every single one of us eliminated one stereotype from our consciousness it wouldn't continue to be perpetuated and would eventually vanish.

Common steps to take, on an individual level, to assess your own stereotypes and eliminate them from your consciousness:

- Respect and appreciate others' differences. Imagine if people looked and acted the same. Boring!
- View people the way you would view flowers in a garden. Each individual is different, unique, yet at the same time and in many ways, quite similar.
- Consider what all people have in common. Lots more than you may realize! We all want a good life, and we have common human needs and desires. And we all face challenges to achieve them.
- Realize that if a person looks different than you, chances are that you probably also look foreign to him or her!

- When tempted to make a snap judgment about someone, ask yourself how you can judge a person you hardly know.
- Avoid making assumptions or creating labels based on superficial traits, like skin or hair color. Someone who looks like an immigrant to you may actually come from a family that has been here longer than yours has!
- Develop empathy for others. Try to walk in their shoes, and imagine how difficult it might be. Realize that your way or the other person's way of thinking or doing something is one of many ways. It is not wrong or right. It is just different.
- Educate yourself. There is plenty of information on the internet. Or just ask the person. Many people love to talk about themselves! Just make sure to be respectful and non-judgmental when you ask.
- Reject negative labels (yours and others') and make it a point to proactively encourage others to do the same.

Summary

It's important to recognize and remember that we all have stereotypes—every single one of us from every corner of the globe. It's part of the human experience. It's not necessarily a positive part of it but a learning experience nonetheless.

That being said, we must remember that as we label others, we too are being labeled. We can let it limit us and those we label or we can rise above it.

The first step is to be honest and recognize our preconceived notions about others, and why we've formed them, and then to take an active approach to educate ourselves.

Points to Ponder:

- Examine your own stereotypes that might be applicable to you. Could they be true? Where did they come from? How do these stereotypes harm you?
- Now think about biases, stereotypes, and prejudices you have about others. Where did they come from? Are they true?
- How can your workplace initiate an honest discussion about stereotypes?
- How may biases and stereotypes have cost your corporation?

Notes

Chapter Seven – Diversity: The Reality

"The real voyage of discovery consists not only in seeking new landscapes but in having new eyes."

-Marcel Proust

Would you ever enter a race with the goal of finishing last or not really caring how you perform during the race?

Would you ever head out to an appointment and not know where you're going and how to get there?

No, right?

Then why would a company institute diversity initiatives and then not follow through? Why would a company adopt a philosophy of diversity and then not dedicate resources and energy to make a change?

It's important at this point in the book to pause and emphasize the importance of diversity in the workforce.

Pause to demonstrate both the present reality and to further emphasize the true benefits of wholeheartedly embracing and supporting diversity and a diverse workforce.

Often, a superficial approach results in mediocre changes to a company's success.

In order to create a whole approach to diversity, meaning every single person in the company from the very top of the pole to the bottom is aligned to support corporate diversity initiatives, a company should include a focus on the following:

1. Be inclusive.
2. Be productive.
3. Be respectful.
4. Commit to the development skills of all people.
5. Embrace and support a team contribution.

This can be accomplished by instituting the initiatives we've discussed in prior chapters, namely:

- Staffing a diverse workforce.
- Gaining a commitment from senior staffers.
- Diversity training and education for all staff members.
- Incorporating input from all employees on diversity initiatives.
- Measures taken to retain employees including training, incentives, respect, and recognition.
- Mentoring programs.
- Strategic efforts to improve corporate image as it relates to diversity.
- Embracing and appealing to a diverse clientele.
- Seeking vendors who support diversity.
- Regular assessment into the overall workplace satisfaction including assessment of satisfaction with diversity progress.

Without committing to all levels of diversity and embracing diversity corporate-wide, companies stand the real chance of failing—of falling short of embracing and supporting their diversity philosophy and being viewed as inconsistent, ineffective, and insincere.

When this happens, the community loses faith in the company and the reputation plummets. This makes it more difficult to recruit top-level talent.

Lack of a serious commitment leads to lost time and money.

It also makes it difficult to retain your talent, and employees are less satisfied, which is directly related to their productivity. The bottom line: neglect to embrace diversity at all levels with a devoted and strategic approach to attaining it, and companies risk losing profits.

In that vein, let's take a look at a few potential pitfalls.

Diversity Pitfalls to Recognize and Avoid

1. Insufficient Training of Officers

Everyone from the top down needs not only diversity training and education but to undergo a serious personal analysis of their attitudes and beliefs about working with others who are different from them.

When this training isn't complete, dissension has the possibility of derailing initiatives. Additionally, people who aren't educated and trained about diversity can create an unpleasant atmosphere.

Often, individuals who lead diversity programs are not fully trained themselves. This wastes company time and money. The result is that the person hires one or two minorities or "diverse employees," believes they've accomplished their goals, and then sits back and relaxes.

The result can be disastrous because new employees are not integrated into the company properly and the guise of diversity becomes nothing more than a sham, leaving employees feeling dissatisfied.

2. Lack of Follow-Up and Evaluation

The only true way to know if a company is on track to achieving their goals is to first evaluate where they stand, set goals and strategies to achieve these goals, and then measure to determine success.

There are many variables to assess and evaluate, including each and every employee's level of satisfaction, both with their work environment and with their perception of diversity initiatives.

3. Management Dropping the Ball

Management needs to do more than create policies and procedures and assume everyone is following through. Part of managing people, and leading them, is to establish policies and procedures to evaluate success.

It's about creating a system of checks and balances, with real repercussions for not following through.

For example, imagine the wasted time and money if management were to pass staffing initiatives onto the Human Resources department without following up to make sure it was happening. Employees would lose faith in management and the result would be an unhappy and unproductive workforce, lack of retention, and in difficulty hiring top-level staff.

4. Lack of a Serious Commitment

Diversity is a buzzword in many businesses/corporations. If a company does not have a serious commitment, the following will become evident:

- Increased disengagement. Employees will feel disconnected from the company and not part of the team.
- Fatigue. Productivity and energy will decrease.
- Disillusionment. A prevailing attitude of "it just doesn't matter" will begin to permeate the consciousness of the employees. They too will begin to not follow through and will lack commitment to the company and company objectives.
- Lack of financial force. Company profits will suffer as employee turnover grows, productivity decreases, and staffing initiatives are derailed because no one wants to be employed by a company with poor employee morale and an inability for management to follow through on initiatives.

Summary

The reality is that diversity is difficult. We're human and there are many variables to manage.

This is why it's so very important for an honest assessment and evaluation to be conducted, goals to be created, strategies implemented to achieve those goals, measurements established to evaluate success, and, of course, recognition for those who achieve diversity goals and repercussions for those who do not.

Diversity needs to be taken seriously.

Businesses that want to succeed in the ever-changing global market need to keep this in mind:

Become Aware, Commit and Embrace Diversity

We've spent an abundant amount of time in this book devoted to recognizing and embracing the amazing benefits a diverse workforce has to offer.

In the next couple of chapters we're going to switch gears and offer tips and strategies for immigrant workers to find employment and for global workers to find a way to work compatibly abroad— namely, understanding the various etiquettes of different cultures.

Points to Ponder:

- Not all diversity initiatives are immediately successful. It takes work, a commitment, and perseverance.
- Lack of a serious commitment dooms companies to failure.
- Support from management is essential for success. It cannot be a bottom-up approach.
- Metrics are essential. How else will you know if you're achieving your goals?
- Training is imperative. We all have our own issues and must be honest about them, learn to communicate effectively, and be educated on diversity.

Notes

Chapter Eight – Breaking Into a New Job Market: New Immigrant Worker

"Men want recognition of their work, to help them to believe in themselves."

-Dorothy Miller Richardson

This chapter takes a different turn. Instead of focusing on companies bettering themselves and positioning themselves to embrace and take advantage of the benefits a diverse workforce offers, I'm turning the tables and we're going to take a look at how immigrants can get the jobs they want. We'll focus on how they can position themselves for success.

We're going to take it on a step-by-step basis as one might do when seeking employment. So what's the first thing you do? You start looking for a job.

Step #1 Beginning the Job Search

If you are of South Asian, Asian, African, Latin, or another ethnic background attempting to go forward with your career, search for a company that treasures diversity. This will give you a good indication whether the company will value your contribution or not.

So Where do You Look for These Companies and These Great Jobs?

Industry Publications

Industry publications are an excellent resource both for finding companies you want to work for and for learning more about companies, which may have job postings.

Targeted Job Boards

The internet is a valuable resource for the job search; however, it's incredibly difficult to get your foot in the door via internet job boards. Websites like Monster.com receive thousands of résumés for each job and, with the economy where it is today, they may be receiving tens of thousands of résumés.

Standing out in that pile of paper is incredibly difficult.

That being said, companies do sometimes recruit from these sites and it can pay to create a profile, post a résumé, and represent yourself online.

Personal and Professional Networks

One of the best ways to find a quality job is through the people you know and through networking. It really pays to put yourself out there. Join organizations that cater to your industry, network, and be proud to introduce yourself to people who are in a position to get you where you want to go.

Once you have a job you wish to apply for, the next step is your résumé.

Step #2 Creating a Powerful, Professional Résumé

There are a few key ingredients for a résumé that's going to capture the attention of hiring managers. These include:

Measurable Accomplishments

Companies want to see not only that you're a good employee, but they want to know that you will provide measurable results for their company. This is demonstrated by having accomplished measurable results for others.

High-Demand Skills

Pick up any industry publication, or for that matter pick up any business publication, and you'll see lists of industries that are in desperate need of skilled professionals. But, more than that, within any industry, there are skills that are specialized, difficult to come by, and in high demand.

Take a moment and consider the industry you're in. What are the in-demand skills required for the positions you're seeking? Do you have these skills? If so, make sure to highlight them on your résumé.

Stable Track Record

Employers are not unrealistic, most of them anyway, and they realize we do not live in a world where we stay in the same job our entire lives. Employers realize that businesses open and close, they realize that people get laid off, and that people leave employers for a variety of reasons.

What they want to see is that you have a stable track record of commitment, dedication, and growth.

Commitment

This will be verified both in your interview, when your potential employer gets to know you a little better, and by your references.

Dedication

The experience that you have stated in your résumé, the experiences that show how you were able to provide benefit to your past employers, will attest to your dedication. Measurable goals cannot be achieved without dedication and commitment. Additionally, your references will be able to attest to this.

Growth

Growth is shown by promotions and career changes with an upward direction. Additionally, salaries can show growth—responsibilities and education or certifications will also show your potential employers that you have the ability to grow.

Personally Qualified

Beyond professional qualifications, companies are looking for personal skills. Communication skills, positive attitudes, leadership skills, teamwork skills, motivation, initiative—the list goes on and on. There are many ways for you to demonstrate your personal qualifications.

By adding leadership, teamwork, or other applicable roles—along with certifications, awards, or accomplishments inside or outside of work—to your résumé, you will demonstrate these skills.

Realistic Expectations

While a fantastic résumé, stellar references, and the best personal skills in the world are outstanding, if you think you should be making a million dollars and have the biggest office and eight weeks vacation, then your expectations may be out of line with your qualifications.

How do you align your expectations with your qualifications?

Salary surveys: Just type the words "salary survey" into any internet search engine and you receive thousands of results. One example is http://www.salary.com.

You also need to research the company you are applying to. Industry reports and publications, local business articles, networking associates, and, of course, your recruiter are all valuable sources of information about your potential employer. Utilize these resources to align your expectation with the available opportunities.

Step #3 The Interview

> "There are no secrets to success. It is the result of preparation, hard work, and learning from failure."
>
> -Colin Powell

So, it all comes to this point. All your research, planning, and hard work have brought you to this one moment to make an impression favourable enough to garner an offer.

One really great way to ease the pressure of this moment is to prepare to the best of your ability.

Here are a few things to consider and steps to take to prepare and put your best foot forward.

Bring Copies of Your Résumé

Bringing extra copies to the interview demonstrates preparedness and it saves time making copies should they bring additional people in on the interview.

Know Your Strengths and Weaknesses

Now it's time for a personal assessment. Grab a pen and a notebook. On one page you'll list your strengths and on the next you'll list your weaknesses.

Now go back to your list and, next to each strength, write a sentence or two on how that strength has been applied to your career and work experiences. Brainstorm how you might discuss these experiences and your strengths with potential employers.

As you did with your strengths, perform the same task with your weaknesses. Brainstorm and plan how you can discuss your weaknesses and how they've presented themselves in your work. Also consider how you can discuss the way you overcome or compensate for your weaknesses.

Turn your weaknesses into strengths. Plan and prepare ahead of time so you can show your prospective employer that while you are aware of your weaknesses, the company will benefit from your strengths and your adaptability.

Practice talking about your strengths, weaknesses, and relevant experiences.

If it has been a while since you've interviewed with anyone, practice ahead of time with a friend or family member. Ask them to give you feedback on your answers.

Visualize your interview ahead of time. Visualizing is a tool Olympic athletes use to achieve their high level of success. You can use it too, to visualize a successful interview.

Imagine the interviewer asking questions and imagine your answers.

Imagine the interview from beginning to end and imagine walking away with a job offer.

Bragging Rights

If there's any time to brag about your skills and accomplishments, it's at an interview.

Often interviews begin with the age-old and dreaded question, "Tell me about yourself."

Your answer to this question will set the tone for the rest of the interview, so it's important to take time to script a positive and impressive answer.

Begin by talking about past experiences and successes. Summarize your career in a sentence or two. From there you can transition into why you like the industry you're in and segue into some of your major accomplishments.

Learn About the Company—And the Interviewer

Collect as much information about the company you're interviewing with as possible. Research online, ask friends and associates.

Educating yourself about the company puts you in a much better position. You'll be able to ask intelligent and relevant questions, you'll be able to focus your answers to fit the company's mission and vision, and you'll demonstrate that you're prepared and passionate about working with the company.

Ask questions! At the end of this section, I have a list of questions you might want to ask your potential employer.

References: A Hiring Manager's Most Useful Tool

Yes, hiring managers give weight to your résumé and to your interview; however, one average or less-than-average reference could make your chances of getting the job go down the drain.

The answer then, of course, is to make sure you have quality verifiable references.

A reference check is an objective evaluation of your past job performances based on conversations with people that you have worked with over the past few years.

Treating references as an afterthought is a careless approach to your job search and it is a sign of carelessness to your potential employer. It shows them that you don't care and that's the opposite of what you want them to think. The best list of references is a mixture of employers, employees, associates, coaches, teachers, co-workers, etc. . . .

Selecting the Best References

- Your references should be from positive people. This is important because individuals that tend to dwell on the negative, even if they are thrilled to be a reference for you, will put a negative twist on everything they say.
- Your references should be both expecting to be contacted and easy to contact. A company is likely to get frustrated if they have to allocate more than a couple of days trying to contact your references. Often it's always a warning sign when a reference is taken aback to be contacted.
- List current references (at least within the past five years) and be sure to list someone that has worked directly with you.
- The absolute best people to list are previous managers and co-workers because they will be able to verbalize on your accomplishments, work ethic, attitude, and more.

Every employer understands that candidates are often dealing with delicate and confidential situations, which means that references can be a touchy situation. There are many ways you can prepare for this situation ahead of time.

How many references do you need?

Employers generally ask for three references; however, because people are often difficult to get a hold of, it is a good idea to have a backup reference.

Make sure to select your references strategically, meaning that if you're applying for a job that requires you to have the ability to develop proposals and you don't really have a work reference that can attest to that, then provide a reference from a community association that you're involved with that can speak on your proposal development skills.

It is important to prepare references ahead of time if you are able to. The best time to coach references is right after the interview and you know more about what the job entails and what types of questions your potential employer is going to ask.

Employers utilize references not only to assure them of your strengths, but they also use your references to clear up any concerns that they may have.

After the interview, hopefully you've gained some insight into what the company is looking for and they've expressed any concerns that they might have about your experience, skills, and background.

Coach your references, if you can, on how to address these concerns. The best companies want references that are happy to be references and are able to provide accurate and detailed information about your professional skills, experience, achievements, work ethic, and much more.

Types of questions your employer may ask your references:

- How are you acquainted with the candidate?
- How long did you work together?
- What was your job title? What was his/her job title?
- What were his/her primary job responsibilities?
- How would you describe the overall job performance?
- How productive was the candidate on the job?
- How would you describe the candidate's attitude?
- Did the candidate have supervisory responsibilities?

- What were the candidate's supervisory responsibilities?
- What were the candidate's strengths? Weaknesses?
- What motivates the candidate?
- Ability to work with others?
- Ability to motivate others?
- Will you describe communication skills, both verbal and written?
- What could the candidate have done to produce better results?
- How would other people describe the candidate?
- What do you think the candidate needs to do to continue to develop professionally?
- Why did the candidate leave the position?
- Would you hire him/her?
- Is there anything else that you'd like to add?

Remember to Be Yourself and to Enjoy the Journey

Remember to have a good time at your interview. If you're prepared and excited about the opportunity it will come through in your actions and facial expressions, and it will be a better experience for everyone. Put yourself in your interviewer's shoes.

Would you rather interview an upbeat, positive person or one who is not excited to be there?

The people you're speaking with are people who have the same hopes, dreams, and fears as everyone else and, like you, they respond well to positive people, to people who are enjoying themselves.

Questions You Might be Asked During Your Interview

Use these questions and topics to prepare for the interview in advance. Consider your answers and position yourself in a positive light.

- Tell me about yourself.
- What is your greatest strength?
- What is your greatest accomplishment?
- What is your greatest weakness?
- What do you like most about your current job?
- What do you like least about your current job?
- Why are you looking to leave?
- How do you approach tasks that you dislike?
- How do you approach tasks that you know you're not strong at?
- Describe some of your current responsibilities.
- Tell me about a time where you had to make an unpopular decision.
- Tell me about the most productive decision you've made.
- Have you ever had to deal with a deadline that you felt was unrealistic and how did you handle that?
- Tell me about a recent problem at work and how you solved it.
- Have you ever had to give bad news to an employee? How did you handle it?
- Describe your communication style.
- How do you prioritize tasks?
- How do you set goals for yourself?
- Describe your organization style.
- Tell me about your ideal work environment.
- Tell me about your ideal job.
- Tell me about a time that you had to deal with a difficult co-worker and how you handled it.
- Tell me about your goals.
- What makes you an ideal candidate for this position?
- What can you offer our company?
- Has anyone ever taken credit for something you've done? How did you handle it?
- What did you do in your last job to improve an area that required improving?
- What do you do to relieve stress?
- How do you handle pressure? How do you define pressure?

Stress?
- What do you find motivating?
- How do you improve the motivation of others?
- What is your description of an ideal supervisor, co-worker, employee, work environment, and work schedule?
- How would you describe yourself as an employee?
- What kind of people do you like to work with?
- What kind of people do you not like to work with?
- How do you feel about your career progress so far?
- What would you avoid in future jobs? Why?
- What aspects of your work give you the greatest satisfaction?
- How do you manage your time?
- What have past employers criticized you for? Praised you for?
- How do you respond when asked to perform a task that is not in your job description?
- What could your previous employers do to convince you to not leave?
- Hypothetical questions are common: For example, "How would you handle an employee who is stealing from the company?"
- What would you say to an employee that challenged your authority?
- How would you avoid conflicts with co-workers? Clients? Employees? Supervisors?
- What is your greatest career accomplishment to date?
- Who or what influences you or has influenced your career goals?
- What is your definition of company loyalty?
- What would your past co-workers say about your performance at your last job? Employees? Supervisors?
- Do you have any questions for me?

Take the time to prepare questions in advance and be sure to take a pen and paper to the interview to record your notes and questions. This makes it easier to keep track of your questions so you don't have to interrupt or lose your train of thought.

It is important to ask questions of your interviewer. This is not only to appear invested in the opportunity but to make sure that, in the event that you do get an offer, you have all of the information necessary to make a proper decision.

Questions to Ask Your Interviewer

- Can you describe the work environment?
- What is the company's overall philosophy?
- What is the company's approach to diversity?
- Are there mentoring and training opportunities?
- What is the management style?
- What are the company's weaknesses and strengths?
- How accessible is senior management by my position and other positions?
- What are some of the short-term objectives you would like to see accomplished in this job?
- What are some of the long-term objectives you would like to see completed?
- How does this position fit within the company's short - and long-term goals?
- How does the company view the issue of work/life balance?
- How does the company view fun in the workplace?
- What are some of the more difficult problems one would have to face in this position?
- What type of support does this position receive in terms of people, finances, etc.?
- What freedom would I have in determining my own work objectives, deadlines, and methods of measurement?
- What advancement opportunities are available for the person who is successful in this position?
- In what ways has this organization been most successful in terms of products and services over the years?
- What significant changes do you foresee in the near future?
- Can you describe a typical day?

- How many hours a week did the incumbent work on average?
- Why did the previous employee leave the job?
- What is the most important aspect of this job?
- What were some of the problems the last incumbent had to face in this job?
- Can you tell me about the person that I would be reporting to?
- Can you describe my co-workers?
- Can you describe the ideal person for this job?
- Who evaluates my job performance?
- What is the first task that I would tackle if I were hired?
- How does this position contribute to the company's goals?
- What are the greatest challenges that I would face in this position?
- How is one evaluated in this position?
- What accounts for success within the company?
- What makes this job an opportunity for me?
- Would I be required to sign a non-compete agreement?
- What are my chances for advancement?
- How does the organization reward performance?
- What is the learning plan for this position?
- How would you compare my skills and experience against other applicants?
- Do you have any concerns about my skills or experience that I can address for you?
- You can ask the interviewer questions about him or herself too. Like, "How long have you worked here?"
- What do you like least and most about working here?
- What advice do you wish someone gave you before you started working here?

Wrapping it Up

Once all your questions have been answered and the interview is coming to a close, make sure that you get names and contact information for all of the people that you have spoken with that day, including any administrative associates that helped you out.

Make sure to be gracious as you exit to all that have been involved with the process, and if you are interested, express that and that you are looking forward to the next step of the process. Interviewers aren't mind readers and this clarification may prove beneficial in their decision-making process. Additionally, leaving on the best note possible is always a good idea.

Don't, however, say too much or lose your professionalism. You may be extremely excited about the opportunity, or vice versa, but the deal isn't done yet and a lot can change with a few inappropriate or unfortunate words. Be gracious. Be professional. Be gone!

A little thank you goes a long way. Few interviewees actually take the time to send a thank you and a note of thanks can be the difference between you getting the job or someone else.

And what about follow-up? Always be sure to inquire about the time line and what the preferred method of follow-up is. Ask them if it's okay for you to call them or if they'd prefer email. And, if the time passes and you haven't heard from them, by all means contact them and inquire. This keeps you in the front of their minds and, while you may not get this opportunity, you will be remembered well and may have a chance of obtaining a different opportunity within the same company.

Here are some tips for a good interview and a positive and productive job search

- **Know your goal:** Your main objective is to show how you fit into the organization and evaluate whether the job is appropriate for you. Additionally, you want to demonstrate the value you can provide the company—they're always thinking about what you can do for them, not the other way around.

- **Do not appear to be too needy:** This will often turn off the interviewer. Of course you want the job—everyone who is interviewing for the position needs the job. However, your need isn't their concern. And if you're focusing more on what they can do for you rather than what you can do for them, you're missing the opportunity.

- **Ineffective non-verbal message:** Illustrate your self-assurance level. Be ready with a smile, stand upright, make eye contact, and offer a strong handshake. Each interview, as cliché as it may sound, brings you one step closer to that ideal job. Approach the interview as an opportunity to learn more and to put your best foot forward—approach it with a positive attitude and it will shine through.

- **Answers only:** While an interview may seem like an inquisition, hiring managers want to know you're engaged and interested in the position. That's demonstrated by asking questions and initiating a dialogue. Instead of only answering questions, try having a conversation with the interviewer.

- **Consider changing or modifying your name so it is easier for people to pronounce:** People don't like to look silly or ignorant and they may feel threatened if you have a difficult name to pronounce. It's okay to pronounce it for them and then let them know what they can call you, if you have a nickname or a modification you go by.

  Often there is a perception that people with ethnic names and education are not familiar with Western culture and have no work experience in the Western culture. To combat this:

  o Consider dressing similarly to the work culture.

  o Understand the Western and work language idioms.

  o Lose your accent. Take professional lessons. Another simple method is to put a pencil across your mouth and read for a minute and then take it out and read aloud. Do this five minutes a day. Your pronunciation will improve dramatically. It is simply retraining the tongue.

- ○ Learn the proper respect of Western culture.

- ○ A strong handshake is a must; look in their eyes and smile.

- ○ Get to know more of the Western culture, whether it is sports, politics, etc.

- ○ Most newly arrived immigrants still have strong ties back home; however, make greater efforts to become familiar with your adopted country.

- **Do not become emotional:** Never become emotional even if the interviewer talks about controversial questions/statements.
- **Leave sensitive and personal issues for another time:** You might feel strongly that you should make your potential employer aware of your needs; for example, your need to take time away to pray several times a day. But your initial interview isn't the right time to address it. (DiversityInc.)
  In fact, according to experts, there is no reason to bring personal obligations or practices up until you've been hired. Once you're hired, employers are obligated to accommodate.
- **Do not babble:** When asking questions, speak in a clear and concise voice to the point. Follow the same guidelines when answering questions. This is a good reason to practice!
- **Listen:** Pay attention to the interviewer before answering questions. If you do not fully understand the question, ask him or her to repeat.
- **Do your homework:** Know about the background of the interviewer and the company. Look up on the internet, utilize industry publications and the media, and don't be afraid to ask people what they know about the company.
- **Asset:** Demonstrate that your coming on board will be an asset to the company.

In an interview with Ms. Gurinder Kang and Nicola Webb, Human Resources Services with the city of Surrey, British Columbia, they offered the following suggestions for candidates who are seeking employment and interviewing for positions:

- One of the biggest mistakes many new immigrant workers make is that they often apply for positions in which they are overqualified for. Often, the employers look at the résumé and say this person is eventually going to leave. Do not undersell yourself.
- Carefully read what the employer is looking for in a job posting. Then use those key words in the cover letter, such as "busy environment . . . fast paced" etc. It is not necessary to add irrelevant information in the application.
- Even if one does not get the job, it is important to call back to get feedback on what they can improve on. Many employers do not mind this. In their home country this might be viewed as "bothering them."
- When it comes to foreign credentials, it is the applicant's duty to prove that it is genuine. Often the employer does not have the resources or the means to search.
- If you are not sure how to apply for a job, contact a non-profit organization to get help.
- If one does not have Canadian work experience, then try volunteering at various non-profit organizations and get references.

Summary

Finding employment is an active process. It begins by positioning yourself within your community, becoming aware of the culture and companies with openings, and positioning yourself well for the opportunity.

Each interview is an opportunity to learn more, become a better interviewee, and to make professional connections. Even if you don't get the job, you're hopefully walking away having made a positive impression and a professional connection, which may help you in the future.

Stay positive!

Points to Ponder:

- What obstacles have you dealt with in the past when applying for positions?
- What learning experiences did you walk away with?
- Take time to practice your interview.
- Take time to research the company and the interviewer.
- Embrace the cultures around you, just as you would like your culture to be respected and embraced.
- What can you do today to modify your résumé to better represent what you have to offer?
- What references do you have? Do you need more?

Notes

Chapter Nine – Etiquettes Abroad

"Good manners will open doors that the best education cannot."

-Clarence Thomas

The future is upon us. Businesses, both online and off, are now employing people from all around the world. Call centers, writing, technology, and a whole host of services can now be outsourced overseas. Additionally, overseas companies are right here in North America employing thousands. Honda, for example, has a huge plant and presence in Ohio.

The point . . .

It's already a global marketplace and, as the trend continues, cultures will mingle and work together toward common causes. In the future it will be the norm for people to work in other parts of world. One-time sleeping nations, China and India, will become super economic powers in the coming years along with Japan. Alone, these three nations consist of over one-third of the world's population: 2 billion plus. Knowing how to conduct yourself is crucial in foreign cultures.

Consider the benefit to your career and your company's productivity and profits if the etiquette of the culture is understood and appreciated.

Imagine the effect it has on you when someone you've just met has put forth the effort to understand your culture's etiquette. Not only is it a recognizable effort, it's a tremendous sign of respect. It immediately puts them in a good light. The same happens when you put forth an effort to understand and appreciate the cultures you're dealing with. It puts you in a good light and gives you an edge. Whether you're selling, negotiating, or simply trying to work together towards a common goal, good things happen when cultures respect and follow etiquette customs.

Here are some of the things to consider.

Asian Cultures:

- Unlike in the Western society, decisions are usually made by the collective groups.
- It is vital first to build relationships—then business.
- Greeting a person is appropriate and slight eye contact is respectful.
- It is not always appropriate to have a strong Western handshake.
- In many parts of Asia, over-touching other professionals can be taboo, especially with the opposite sex. It's better to view other professional associates in your group and follow suit.
- Anticipate business to be completed in a leisurely manner. Rushed business tends to be viewed as highly suspect.
- Do less speaking and more listening.
- Position of status is very important. Be aware as to who is who.

India:

- It's important to shake hands or greet with both hands which is called "Namaste." Bring both hands together and raise them to your forehead and slowly bring them down. This is hello and goodbye.
- Shaking hands: Only do this if you are male greeting another male. Shake a female's hands only if she extends her hand first. The same rule applies if you are a female greeting a male. A female shaking the hand of another female is acceptable.
- Before getting down to business, small chit chat is appropriate. They may want to know your personal background regarding family and education. Keep it light. Family is very important.
- You must build trust first—before any type of business can be carried out.
- Avoid discussing religion and politics, as they could be touchy topics.
- At dinner: when invited by a Hindu, Sikh, or Muslim person: wait until they invite you to eat.

- You must eat something even if you are full. Not eating is a sign of disrespect.
- Try using the right hand. Use a serving spoon when serving yourself.
- It is unacceptable for you to serve others with your utensils.
- It is okay to pass the dishes with your left hand supported by your right hand.
- Your drinking glass can be raised with your left hand as well.
- Often you are offered a small dish with warm water to clean your finger tips.
- Gift offering is much more acceptable in Japan than in China or India.
- Greeting individuals with their titles is viewed as respect. (Dr., Professor, etc.)
- South Asian dress code is slightly more formal than Western. It's important that females are dressed properly.
- Consider printing one side of your business card in English and the other side in the Asian language. When presenting your card, present it with the Asian language side up and hold the card with both hands.
- In most places English is used as the working language.
- Do not get upset when marital or personal family questions arise.

China:

- Building relationships is vital.
- When given, receive business card with both hands. Read the card and acknowledge it.
- Position business cards in front of you, if seated at a large table—it's a representation of respect.
- Use basic Chinese characters, not classical characters from Hong Kong or Taiwan.
- Have your business card printed in English/Cantonese or Mandarin.

- Business gifts should be reciprocated.
- Chinese people refuse gifts several times before accepting.
- Make sure your gift is of higher quality.
- Gifts should preferably be chosen based on their coming in two, such as a set of something.
- Acknowledgment for hierarchy is important.
- Business partners should not be called by their first names—it's a lack of respect.
- To write in red ink symbolizes the writer will depart in this life.
- Chinese people are superstitious. Try not use the number 4—it means death.
- Do not be offended when questions about marriage arise.
- During a meal, never place chop sticks in a rice bowl.

These basic guidelines may seem inconsequential to you; however, understanding, appreciating, and following the etiquette and customs of the people you're doing business with can only bring about good results. And you'll probably learn something in the process.

Points to Ponder:

- Which cultures do you do business with? Do you understand the culture? Do you know the etiquettes?
- Do you understand and recognize the benefits of adopting the local customs and etiquettes? When in Rome, as they say.
- What can you do to further educate yourself on the etiquettes and customs of the people you do business with?

Notes

Chapter Ten – Ideal Business Climate in the Twenty-First Century

"We all live with the objective of being happy; our lives are all different and yet the same."

-Anne Frank

Imagine a workplace where . . .

People over the age of 65 are working into their 80s—due to good health and financial considerations.

Ethnic racial minorities are well represented in all levels of the company; companies have very little choice due to shrinking of Western workforce.

Bias-free attitudes prevail in most companies and corporations due to better education as well as traveling and working abroad.

Greater religious tolerance and awareness is present in all workplaces—due to ongoing global urbanization.

There's an equal distribution of men and women, with women wanting greater independence, especially at professional levels.

Sexual attitudes and differences are accepted and respected.

Work mobility equals technical advances, making it easier to telecommute or work in other countries.

All companies embrace elevated social and community obligations. For example, Bill Gates gives millions of dollars to various humanitarian causes.

There's a greater emphasis for research and development in various categories from health to science, etc.

All companies actively participate and give back to their communities at local levels; they're respected, acknowledged, and supported by community.

All of this—and more—isn't only possible, it's probable.

In order to survive and be competitive in the twenty-first century, companies have to embrace and support a diverse workforce.

The ideal business climate companies should be striving for is one that addresses:

The current demographics. When a workforce is out of sync with the world around it, progress and innovation are stunted. However, when the workforce reflects the outside world, business owners and managers are better in tune with trends and thus ready to adapt, innovate, and prosper. They're able to position themselves competitively with consumers around the world and build relationships with suppliers.

The power of innovation and creativity. Men and women of all ages, religions, ethnic backgrounds, races, sexual orientation, disabilities, skills, and various levels of education work together to bring about a dynamic workforce. This creates a fertile breeding ground for thoughts, ideas, opinions, and even systems of beliefs to improve and grow a business.

The expectations of customers. Based on demographics changes, where we work, what we do, and whom we do it with continues to shift along with who provides the service, what the service is, and how the service is provided. A diverse workforce enables you to stay in tune with changes and adapt quickly.

Evolving technologies. Technology is evolving constantly and we must change accordingly.

Broadening horizons and globalization. An ideal workforce is one that views diversity as an opportunity. A diverse workforce has its finger on the pulse of the consumer.

Diverse suppliers. Embracing diversity with your suppliers helps build relationships and, in business, those who have strong partnerships are the ones that survive and thrive.

In the workplace of the twenty-first century, diversity is about more than affirmative action. It's about understanding biases, our own and others', it's about dialogue, education, compassion, and a true effort to change corporate missions, visions, and strategies.

As the world shrinks and globalization prevails, the need for diversity will increase significantly in the coming years.

Successful organizations recognize the need for immediate action and are ready and willing to spend resources on managing diversity in the workplace now. Are you?

When your company embraces diversity from the top down and creates the workforce of the future, you will:

- Attract, recruit, and retain people from a wide "talent" base.
- Reduce the costs of labor turnover, productivity, and absenteeism.
- Gain better employee flexibility and responsiveness.
- Increase employee commitment and morale.
- Enhance creativity and innovation.
- Improve knowledge of how to operate effectively in different cultures.
- Improve the understanding of the needs of current customers.
- Improve company knowledge about the needs of new customers.
- Develop new products, services, and marketing strategies.
- Enhance your reputation and image within your community.

The Key is to Make Workplace Diversity a Priority

Your success and ability to compete in an increasingly global market depends on your ability to embrace diversity and realize the benefits.

As we've discussed throughout this book, it begins with the very top-level managers and employees and trickles down to include each and every employee. It's about changing policies and procedures to support diversity, it's about education, and it's about assessment and evaluation.

We're each independently responsible for making a larger change. It begins by assessing and discussing our own personal beliefs, biases, and stereotypes. It begins with honesty. And it ends with prosperity and a global and diverse workforce that supports innovation, recognition, and growth.

An organization that embraces diversity at its core receives:

- An ability to adapt quickly to changes in the marketplace.
- An ability to offer products and services to a broader clientele.
- An ability to tap into creativity and innovation.
- An ability to execute and respond quickly and appropriately to challenges.

Businesses that want to succeed in the ever-changing global market need to keep this in mind:

Become **Aware, Commit and Embrace**.

124

Notes

Conclusions

1. If a company's bases are global as well as diverse, they will have a better chance of being successful. Greater diversity means greater competitiveness.
2. It is crucial to be able to relate to other cultures and markets, which is a strong point for any company if they want to succeed in the global market.
3. Conference Board released a study that suggests an ethnically diverse workforce can make a company more profitable.
4. For any company to succeed in the twenty-first century, companies must have a knowledge and understanding of what it means to be diverse and what it means to embrace diversity.
5. The face of the Western workforce will become more diverse; however, it won't happen by itself. Leaders who believe in and see the benefit of diversity must lead the way. Initiatives must be implemented and long-term policies must be put into place.
6. To be effective and to grow, thrive, and prosper, management needs to recognize, respect, and capitalize on different ethnic backgrounds.
7. Hiring and retaining an ethnic staff allows companies to serve broad bases of clients around the world with ease.

Appendix & Checklist

1. What are your organization's top diversity goals and objectives?

_____

_____

_____

_____

_____

2. What processes are currently in place to achieve your organization's diversity goals and objectives?

Some possibilities include:

- Mentoring.
- Training.
- Recruitment.
- Management involvement.
- Regular inclusion of diversity topics at meetings.
- Recognition of diversity champions.
- Community involvement and outreach.

_____

_____

_____

_____

_____

3. If you have diversity processes in place, are the systems or initiatives working? Why or why not?

_____

_____

_____

_____

_____

4. Does your organization have a diversity strategy? If so, what is it? Is it incorporated in your company philosophy, and its vision and mission statements?

_____
_____
_____
_____
_____

5. Does your company measure diversity initiatives and strategies for effectiveness? If yes, how and what do you measure?

_____
_____
_____
_____
_____

6. Is your organization's diversity strategy incorporated into your organizational core values, strategic plans, and performance indicators?

_____
_____
_____
_____
_____

7. Does your organization have a budget to support its diversity strategy?

_____
_____
_____
_____
_____
_____

8. What does senior leadership do to demonstrate its commitment to diversity?

_____
_____
_____
_____
_____
_____
_____

9. Do you measure diversity indicators?

_____
_____
_____
_____
_____
_____

10. Do you measure employee satisfaction, overall and with diversity issues and initiatives?

_____
_____
_____
_____
_____
_____
_____
_____
_____
_____

11. Are you aware of your own personal biases and stereotypes?

_____
_____
_____
_____
_____
_____
_____
_____

12. Do you have formal and/or informal mentoring programs?

_____
_____
_____
_____
_____
_____
_____

13. Do you have diversity training and education programs?

_____
_____
_____
_____
_____
_____
_____
_____

14. Do you promote and support honest dialogue about biases, stereotypes, and perceptions?

_____

_____

_____

_____

_____

_____

_____

15. Do you have strategic recruitment policies in place to hire a diverse workforce?

_____

_____

_____

_____

_____

_____

_____

16. Do you have strategic retention policies and strategies in place to keep employees?

_____

_____

_____

_____

_____

_____

_____

Resources

- *Making Diversity Work: 7 Steps for Defeating Bias in the Workplace,* Sondra Thiederman, PH.D.
- *When Generations Collide: Who They Are. Why They Clash. How to Solve the Generational Puzzle at Work,* Lynne C Lancaster and David Stillman.
- *Generations at Work: Managing the Clash of Veterans, Boomers, Xers, and Nexters in Your Workplace,* Ron Zemke, Claire Raines Bob Filipczak.
- *Diversity Leaders Not Labels: A New Plan for the 21st Century,* Stedman Graham.
- Diversityinc.com.
- NC State University Office For Equal Opportunity Guidelines for Recruiting a Diverse Workforce.
- U.S. Department of Commerce Best Practices in Achieving Workforce Diversity.
- WorkplaceDiversity.com.

CPSIA information can be obtained
at www.ICGtesting.com
Printed in the USA
LVOW03s1411070317
526300LV00002B/3/P

9 781933 817606